Get Together

Susan Iannuzzi • David McKeegan

with Mirna Züge

OXFORD

UNIVERSITY PRESS

Contents

	GRAMMAR	VOCABULARY	FUNCTIONS	FOCUS
Unit 9 **There were temples at the Acropolis.** Page 41	Simple past with *be*: affirmative and negative statements Common past time words	Silverware and other table items	Comparing the past and present Talking about history	**Listening:** A comparison of past and present **Speaking and Writing:** An interview and a description of a town in the past
Unit 10 **Where were the schools?** Page 45	Simple past of *be*: *yes/no* questions and short answers; information questions	Farm animals	Asking and answering questions about history and past events	**Reading:** *The Persian Rider* **Speaking:** Animals of the past
Rewind Units 9 & 10				
Unit 11 **We fixed the walls.** Page 51	Simple past of regular and irregular verbs: affirmative and negative statements	Irregular verbs	Talking about the past	**Reading:** A "to do" list **Writing:** A diary entry
Unit 12 **What did you see in Greece?** Page 55	Simple past of regular and irregular verbs: *yes/no* questions and short answers; information questions	Irregular verbs	Asking and answering questions about the past	**Speaking and Writing:** A description of a trip
Rewind Units 11 & 12				
Unit 13 **He was acting strangely.** Page 61	Past progressive: affirmative and negative statements	Verbs related to moving to a new house	Talking about events in the past	**Reading:** A conversation **Writing:** What was I doing...?
Unit 14 **Where were you playing?** Page 65	Past progressive: *yes/no* questions and short answers; information questions	Accessories	Asking and answering questions about past events *That's awful / great!* *I think...*	**Speaking and Writing:** Charades: What was I doing...?
Rewind Units 13 & 14				
Unit 15 **We were playing when he found it.** Page 71	*When* and *while* Comparison of past progressive and simple past	Forms of transportation	Talking about something that was happening in the past and was interrupted by another action	**Listening:** A press conference **Writing:** A story
Unit 16 **Speedy is our hero!** Page 75	Review: verb tenses	Banquet foods	Talking about the past	**Reading:** An official's speech **Writing:** A description of a party
Rewind Units 15 & 16				

Unit 1

They report for *Explore the World.*

(1) 🎧 **Read quickly. Label pictures 1-3 with the captions below. Then listen.**

Iman and a lion cub　　　　The reporters　　　　Brad and his dad

1 ___The reporters___　　2 _____　　3 _____

Jay Jones and Yvonne Simms
Jay and Yvonne report for *Explore the World*, your favorite magazine and TV show! Yvonne is our teen reporter. She talks to teenagers from all around the world. Here are her reports on two international teens.

Brad Westwood
Brad Westwood lives in Hollywood, California. His father is a stuntman in action movies. Stuntmen do dangerous things for the actors. Brad knows some famous actors. He goes to school with John Hunter's daughters.

Iman Onuku
Iman Onuku is Kenyan. Her mother is a veterinarian. Vets help sick animals. Iman and her family live near Meru National Park. In this picture, Iman is playing with a lion cub.

1

Got it?

(2) **Read the magazine page in exercise 1 again. Answer the questions.**

1 Who is the teen reporter for *Explore the World*?　—　___Yvonne.___

2 Who knows famous actors?　—　_____

3 Who lives near Meru National Park?　—　_____

Focus on language!

Review: simple present and present progressive

SIMPLE PRESENT	PRESENT PROGRESSIVE
I **sing**.	I am **singing** right now.
I **do not/don't sing**.	I am **not singing** right now.
What **do** you **eat** for breakfast?	What **are** you **eating** now?
What **does** he/she **watch** on TV?	What **is** he/she **watching** now?

statements

information questions

Use the simple present for daily habits and usual activities.
Use the present progressive for actions that are/are not happening right now.

③ Circle the correct verb form in parentheses.

1 Yvonne (*interviews* / *interview*) teens for *Explore the World*.

2 Yvonne (*is talking* / *are talking*) to Jay right now.

3 Yvonne's parents (*writes* / *write*) for a magazine, but they (*doesn't work* / *don't work*) for *Explore the World*.

4 Yvonne's sisters (*am singing* / *are singing*) at school today.

5 Yvonne (*plays* / *play*) the piano, but she (*doesn't sing* / *don't sing*).

④ Write the correct short forms of the verbs in parentheses.

1 Brad ___doesn't live___ in New York. He lives in California.
   (*not / live*)

2 Brad's father _____ an easy job.
   (*not / have*)

3 Brad's father _____ right now. He is doing stunts.
   (*not / watch TV*)

4 Brad's parents _____ pizza.
   (*not / like*)

⑤ Fill in the blanks with the simple present or the present progressive forms of the verbs in parentheses.

I'm Iman Onuku. I ___live___ (**1** *live*) in Kenya. My mother is a vet

and my father is a history teacher. My father _____ (**2** *teach*) at

my school, but he _____ (**3** *not / teach*) my class today.

A lion cub _____ (**4** *live*) with us. It _____

(**5** *sleep*) right now because it's tired. It usually _____

(**6** *sleep*) in the morning. It _____ (**7** *not / sleep*) in the house.

6 Write the questions. Use the words in parentheses and the simple present or present progressive.

1 <u>Where does Iman live?</u>   — She lives in Kenya.
            (Where / Iman)

2 _____ — He teaches at her school.
            (Where / Iman's father)

3 _____ — It is sleeping right now.
            (What / the lion cub)

4 _____ — It usually sleeps in the morning.
            (When / the lion cub)

7 🎧 Listen to Yvonne's interview with Brad. Number the pictures.

A = _____   B = _____   C = _____   D = __1__

8 Look at the photos below. Match the objects in the second row (*A-D*) to the professions in the first row (*1-4*).

1 mail carrier – _C_   2 shopkeeper – ___   3 hairdresser – ___   4 photographer – ___

A cash register   B camera   C mail bag   D scissors

9 Fill in the blanks with the words in the box.

| shopkeeper | mail carrier | photographer | hairdresser |

1 Erika uses scissors. She works with hair. Erika is a _____hairdresser_____ .

2 Oscar sells things. Oscar is a _____ .

3 Martin knows all the addresses in his city. He is a _____ .

4 Chung's photographs are in magazines. Chung is a _____ .

10 Work in pairs. You are a reporter. Your partner is a guest on the guest list below. Role-play an interview.

Example   REPORTER: What's your name?
            GUEST: My name is Midori Sato.
      REPORTER: What do you do?
            GUEST: I'm a photographer.
      REPORTER: Where do you live?
            GUEST: I live in Osaka.

GUEST LIST

NAME	JOB	LIVES IN...
Midori Sato	photographer	Osaka
Joe Bates	reporter	Dublin
Sue Simms	vet	San Diego
Angelo Murad	shopkeeper	Ottawa

In your notebook, write a short report about each guest.

Example   This is Midori Sato. She's a photographer. She lives in Osaka.

Put it together!

11 Interview three classmates about people in their families. Complete the chart.

Example   What's your aunt's name?   —   Her name is Susan.
          What does your aunt do?   —   She's a teacher.
          Where does your aunt live?   —   She lives in Atlanta.

Classmate's name	Name of person in classmate's family	Job	Town/City
1 John	Susan	teacher	Atlanta
2			
3			
4			

It's older than I am!

1 🎧 **Read quickly. Guess the meanings of the words. Circle *a* or *b*. Then listen.**

1 *junk* = **a** important things   **2** *treasures* = **a** important things
          b useless things   **b** useless things

JAY: Welcome to *Explore the World*. Today I'm visiting shopkeeper Seymour Sassoon in New York. Seymour collects and sells...um...junk from all over the world!

SEYMOUR: No, Jay, these things aren't <u>useless</u> junk. They're useful treasures. Some of them are very expensive.

JAY: Oh, sorry. Hmm...this elephant statue is interesting.

SEYMOUR: Yes, it's from India.

JAY: Wow, it's really fat! Hey, that box is as big as the elephant, but it's more colorful. I love it.

SEYMOUR: Yes, it's beautiful. It's from Japan. It's 80 years old.

JAY: Wow! It's older than I am! And it's cheap! It's only $35!

SEYMOUR: $35? Sorry, Jay...it's $3,500!

Got it?

2 **Underline the adjectives in the conversation, as in the example in line 3 above.**

3 **Read the conversation again. Answer the questions. Use short answers.**

1 Who is Jay interviewing?   —   <u>Seymour Sassoon</u>

2 Where is the elephant from?   —   _____

3 How much is the colorful box?   —   _____

Focus on language!

Comparative: short adjectives

Rule 1 Most adjectives: + -er
small → small**er**

Rule 2 Adjectives ending in -e: + -r
nice → nice**r**

Rule 3 Adjectives ending in consonant + -y:
-y → -i + -er
heavy → heav**ier**

Rule 4 Adjectives ending in a vowel and a consonant: double consonant + -er
big → bi**gger**

NOTE: Comparative sentences usually use *than*. Sue is **taller than** Jack.

4 Study Rules 1, 2, 3, and 4 in the grammar chart. Then change the adjectives below to make comparative forms.

Rule 1	small*er*	tall_____	cold_____
Rule 2	nice*r*	large_____	cute_____
Rule 3	heavy/*ier*	tiny_____	sunny_____
Rule 4	big*ger*	fat_____	hot_____

5 Look at the clocks in Seymour's shop. Fill in the blanks with the comparative forms of *heavy, big, long, small,* and *old*.

1 The gray clock is _____smaller than_____ the white clock.

2 The red clock is _____ the blue clock.

3 The brown clock is _____ the white clock.

4 The white clock is _____ the brown clock.

5 The brown clock is _____ the gray clock.

6 **Look at the pictures.**

clean

dirty

quiet

noisy

soft

hard

Now write *O (Opposites)* or *N/O (Not opposites)*.

1 dirty / clean   <u>O</u>

2 quiet / hard   <u>N/O</u>

3 hard / noisy   _____

4 soft / hard   _____

5 noisy / quiet   _____

6 clean / soft   _____

7 **Write sentences. Use the correct form of the adjectives in parentheses.**

1 <u>The plates are cleaner than the cups.</u>
    (the plates / the cups) (clean)

2 _____
    (the cups / the plates) (dirty)

3 _____
    (the chair / the sofa) (hard)

4 _____
    (the sofa / the chair) (soft)

5 _____
    (the concert hall / the library) (noisy)

6 _____
    (the library / the concert hall) (quiet)

Comparative: long adjectives

famous → **more** famous **than**   colorful → **more** colorful **than**
useful → **more** useful **than**   interesting → **more** interesting **than**
difficult → **more** difficult **than**   beautiful → **more** beautiful **than**

8 Fill in the blanks with the comparative form of the adjectives. Use *more...than*.

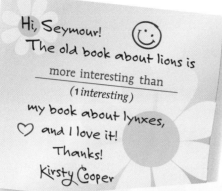

Hi, Seymour! ☺
The old book about lions is
<u>more interesting than</u>
(1 interesting)
my book about lynxes,
♡ and I love it!
Thanks!
Kirsty Cooper

Dear Seymour,
I love the Indian elephant statue! It's
_____ my
(2 beautiful)
statues from Italy. And the new
plates are _____
my old plates.   (3 colorful)
Thanks!
Paola Avitelli

from the desk of Jay Jones

EXPLORE *the* WORLD!

Seymour! Our interview is on TV tonight!
You're _____ I am now!
(4 famous)
I remember that Japanese box! It's
beautiful, but it's _____
(5 expensive)
my car! See you!   Jay Jones

Tip

Use *as...as* for equal things.

The camera is **as heavy as** the radio.

9 Look at the Tip and the picture below. Fill in the blanks with *as...as* and the correct adjective.

| expensive | old | colorful | big |

1 The red mask is <u>as big as</u> the white mask.

2 The small box is _____
the red mask.

3 The large box is _____ the small box.

4 The red mask is _____
the white mask.

Put it together!

10 Work in pairs. Where do you want to go on vacation? Choose your favorite place. Compare your favorite place with your partner's favorite place. Write sentences in your notebook. Use adjectives like *hot/cold*, *interesting/boring*, and *cheap/expensive*.

Example   Toronto is colder than Miami. Toronto is...

Rewind —— Units 1&2

① Put the verbs in parentheses into the simple present.

This is Jee Wha. She ___lives___ in Seoul, South Korea. She _____ a
(**1** *live*)   (**2** *have*)

brother and a sister. They all _____ to the same school. Their father
(**3** *go*)

is an actor, and their mother _____ for a newspaper. She _____
(**4** *write*)   (**5** *leave*)

her office at 5 P.M. every day. Jee Wha _____ Korean and English at
(**6** *study*)

school, but she _____ French. They _____ French at Jee Wha's school.
(**7** *not / study*)   (**8** *not / teach*)

② Read the paragraph again and answer the questions. Use short answers.

1 Does Jee Wha live in Seoul? — Yes, she does.

2 Do Jee Wha's parents have two children? — _____

3 Does Jee Wha's father work in a bank? — _____

4 Does Jee Wha's mother work in the evening? — _____

5 Do Jee Wha and her family speak Korean? — _____

③ Match the questions about Jee Wha with the answers.

1 Where do Jee Wha and her family live?   **A** At 5 P.M.
2 What does Jee Wha's father do?   **B** Jee Wha's mother.
3 When does Jee Wha's mother finish work?   **C** Korean and English.
4 What does Jee Wha study at school?   **D** In Seoul.
5 Who writes for a newspaper?   **E** He's an actor.

④ Label the objects in the pictures. Then match them with the professions.

1 __cash register__   **2** _____   **3** _____   **4** _____

shopkeeper __1__   hairdresser ____   mail carrier ____   photographer ____

⑤ Fill in the blanks with the correct comparative form.

1 hard	_harder_	soft	_softer_	quiet	_quieter_
2 large	_____	nice	_____	cute	_____
3 hot	_____	big	_____	fat	_____
4 dirty	_____	noisy	_____	happy	_____
5 beautiful	_____	expensive	_____	difficult	_____

⑥ Write sentences about Bob and Bill. Use the comparative forms of the words in parentheses.

1 Bill _____is older than_____ Bob.
(*old*)

2 Bob _____ Bill.
(*short*)

3 Bill _____ Bob.
(*heavy*)

4 Bill _____ Bob.
(*tall*)

5 Bob _____ Bill.
(*thin*)

6 Bill's hair _____ Bob's hair.
(*long*)

Bob   Bill

⑦ First, find 15 adjectives in the word square. Then use some of the adjectives to write comparative sentences in your notebook about the groups below.

A	B	R	A	N	C	H	E	A	P	S
F	T	P	R	O	O	B	R	H	N	B
R	H	B	I	G	L	F	A	O	U	E
O	I	F	R	E	D	A	S	T	H	A
B	N	R	A	T	O	N	G	O	E	U
D	A	N	G	E	R	O	U	S	A	T
I	Q	U	I	E	T	I	S	F	V	I
R	S	S	H	O	A	S	O	N	Y	F
T	O	P	S	O	L	Y	O	U	N	U
Y	F	U	S	T	L	S	M	A	L	L
S	T	E	X	P	E	N	S	I	V	E

1 lion, elephant, dog

2 Brazil, Australia, Japan

3 car, bus, bicycle

Example

A dog is smaller than a lion.

A lion is more dangerous than a dog.

An elephant is as beautiful as a lion.

Unit 3 It's the highest mountain in the world.

(1) 🎧 **Read quickly. Where are they? Fill in the blanks. Then listen.**

1 Yvonne's in _____.

2 Jay's in _____.

YVONNE: Hi! *Explore the World* is in two special places today! I'm here in Rio de Janeiro, Brazil. Brazil has some of the best beaches in South America, and for me, the people here are the friendliest in the world! Hey, Jay. Are you there?

JAY: Yes, I am! Good evening, everyone! I'm in Nepal. For me, this is the most incredible place in the world. Look, there's Mount Everest behind me! It's the highest mountain in the world. The world's strongest climbers come here every year. Oh, here's my guide! See you later.

Got it?

(2) **Read the conversation again. Circle the correct answers.**

1 What is Mount Everest?

   a A beach.   **b** A mountain.   **c** A country.

2 Where is Mount Everest?

   a In Nepal.   **b** In Brazil.   **c** In South America.

3 Where is Rio de Janeiro?

   a In Brazil.   **b** On Mount Everest.   **c** In Nepal.

Focus on language!

Superlative: short adjectives

Rule 1 Most adjectives: + -est
small → small**est**

Rule 2 Adjectives ending in -e: + -st
nice → nic**est**

Rule 3 Adjectives ending in -y: -y → -i + -est
heavy → heav**iest**

Rule 4 Adjectives ending in a vowel and a consonant: double consonant + -est
big → bi**ggest**

NOTE: Begin superlative expressions with *the*.
Sue is **the tallest** girl in the class.

3 Fill in the blanks with the correct superlative form.

1 hot — the hottest
2 happy — _____
3 tall — _____
4 strong — _____
5 big — _____
6 heavy — _____
7 large — _____
8 long — _____
9 cold — _____

4 Read the magazine page. Fill in the blanks with the correct form of *tall, cold, old,* and *long*.

EXPLORE the WORLD!

1 The Great Wall of China is ___the longest___ wall in the world. Many people visit the Wall, but not many people walk from one end to the other!

2 The _____ building in the world is the Petronas Towers in Kuala Lumpur, Malaysia. Don't look down!

3 The Sakkara Pyramid is _____ pyramid in Egypt. It's 4,500 years old!

4 The South Pole in Antarctica is _____ place on earth. It can be -100° C !

Superlative: long adjectives

beautiful → **the most** beautiful   famous → **the most** famous

5 **Match the words with the letters on the map.**

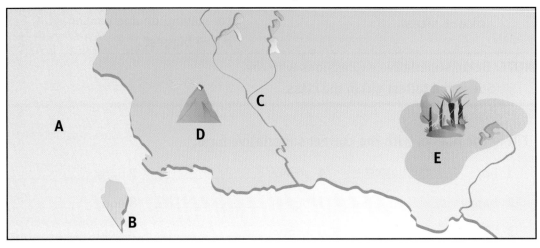

volcano D   river ___   rain forest ___   ocean ___   island ___

6 **What does Yvonne think? Write sentences for her report. Put the words in parentheses in the correct order. Use the superlative form. Do you agree with her?**

1   The Atlantic is the most famous ocean in the world.
          (The Atlantic / ocean / famous / in the world)

2   _____
          (Mount Pinatubo / volcano / dangerous / in Asia)

3   _____
          (Hawaii / island / colorful / in the Pacific Ocean)

4   _____
          (The Amazon / rain forest / exciting / in the world)

5   _____
          (The Nile / river / important / in Africa)

7 **Fill in the blanks with the superlative forms of the words in parentheses.**

Welcome to Mount Everest! It's ___the highest___ mountain
                                    (1 *high***)**

in the world and _____ place in Nepal! It's also
                          (2 *beautiful***)**

_____ place in Asia! Sukra, my guide, is
        (3 *cold***)**

_____ and _____ man on Mount Everest!
  (4 *strong***)**   **(5** *friendly***)**

8 **Read Yvonne's interview with Dr. Gray.**

YVONNE: Hi, everyone. This is the best vet in the world, George Gray! He helps wild animals!

GEORGE: Thanks, Yvonne! But I'm not the best vet. There are lots of great vets in the world.

YVONNE: You have many interesting animals here! Is that yellow snake a python?

GEORGE: Yes, it is! Pythons are the longest snakes in the world. And they're the strongest snakes in the world, too!

YVONNE: What's the best food for pythons? Do they like candy?

GEORGE: No! Candy is the worst food for them. Pythons eat small animals.

YVONNE: What's that green snake in the water?

GEORGE: That's an anaconda. The anaconda is one of the most dangerous snakes in the world.

Tip

	Comparative	Superlative
good →	better than →	the best
bad →	worse than →	the worst

Some adjectives are irregular.

Now write P (Python) or A (Anaconda).

1 Green snake = <u>A</u>

2 The longest snake = __

3 The most dangerous snake = __

4 The strongest snake = __

9 **In your notebook, write sentences about the snakes in exercise 8. Use comparative forms.**

Example Pythons are longer than anacondas.

Put it together!

10 **You are a tour guide. Recommend places in your city or town to a visitor. Write a paragraph in your notebook. Then compare your paragraph with a partner's paragraph.**

Example New York City is great. The best park in our city is…. The most famous statue is….

Unit 4

The people cheer noisily.

1 **Read quickly. What is the Olympic Village? Circle *a* or *b*. Then listen.**

a A home for athletes at the Olympic Games.　　**b** A big city.

EXPLORE *the* WORLD!

Athletes from all over the world compete in the Olympic Games. These athletes always stay in the Olympic Village. The Olympic Village has many shops and restaurants. The athletes can run easily from one end of the Village to the other. Some athletes do this every day for training!

The Olympic Village is an exciting place, too. At night, the tired athletes sleep quietly, but other people dance and cheer noisily in the streets. The Olympic Village is a great place for parties!

Jay and Yvonne are reporting from the Olympic Village this week. Watch them on Explore the World *on Wednesday at 8 P.M.*

4

Got it?

2 **Read the magazine page again. Circle *T* (*True*) or *F* (*False*).**

1 Athletes compete in the Olympic Games.	(T)/ F
2 Athletes don't run in the Olympic Village.	T / F
3 The Olympic Village is a boring place.	T / F
4 There aren't any parties in the Olympic Village.	T / F
5 *Explore the World* is on Wednesday at 8 P.M.	T / F

Focus on language!

Regular adverbs

Rule 1 Adjective + -*ly*
quiet + -*ly* → quiet**ly**
I sing **quietly**.

Rule 2 Adjective ending in -*y*: -*y* → -*i* + -*ly*
happy: -*y* → -*i* + -*ly* → happ**ily**
We cheer **happily**.

3 **Circle the adverbs. Some sentences do not have adverbs.**

1 The Mexicans are cheering (noisily) for their team. They are very happy.

2 The Chinese team is performing wonderfully.

3 The Olympic Village is a wonderful place.

4 Yvonne and Jay are good reporters.

5 This tennis team is winning easily.

6 I can't sit quietly at the Olympics!

4 **Fill in the blanks with the adverb. Use the adjective in parentheses.**

YVONNE: Oh, my ears! The Italians are cheering really __noisily__ for their athletes.
(**1** *noisy*)

JAY: Yes, they are! Their athletes are performing _____. Their teams
(**2** *wonderful*)

are winning _____ ! The Australian teams are also performing
(**3** *easy*)

_____ .
(**4** *beautiful*)

YVONNE: Yes! Look at that Australian runner. He's smiling _____ !
(**5** *happy*)

He's winning the race!

Irregular adverbs

ADJECTIVE	ADVERB	EXAMPLES (adjective — adverb)	
fast	fast	I am a **fast** reader.	– I read **fast**.
early	early	I take an **early** bus.	– I get up **early**.
late	late	He is **late** for school.	– He goes to school **late**.
good	well	She is a **good** player.	– She plays **well**.

5 **Underline the adjectives. Circle the adverbs.**

Ludmila plays on a <u>great</u> volleyball team. She gets up (early) every day. She never wakes up late. She takes an early bus to the stadium. Ludmila plays volleyball well. She can run fast. She is strong. She is a good athlete.

6 **Look at the pictures and labels. Then write sentences. Use the words in parentheses.**

gymnast

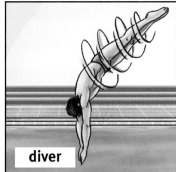
diver

runners

1 <u>The gymnast is jumping gracefully.</u>
　　　　　(gymnast / jump / gracefully)

2 _____
　　　　　(diver / turn / quickly)

3 _____
　　　　　(runner in red / run / slowly)

7 **Fill in the blanks with adjectives or adverbs. Use the words in parentheses.**

1 Tanya is a _____graceful_____ gymnast.
　　　　　　(graceful)

2 The Americans are swimming _____ today.
　　　　　　　　　　　(quick)

3 That football player is very _____ .
　　　　　　　　　　(fast)

4 Those women dance very _____ .
　　　　　　　　　　(graceful)

5 The old men walk _____ .
　　　　　　　(slow)

8 🎧 **Look at the pictures. Listen to the dialog. Fill in the chart.**

Name	Age	Score	Graceful dancer?	Good jumper?
Olga Korman	15			
Mary Rizon			yes	no
Dana Stoico		9.66		

9 **Look at the chart in exercise 8. Answer the questions.**

1 Who is the highest scorer? <u>Olga.</u>

2 Who is the oldest gymnast? _____

3 Who is the worst dancer? _____

10 **Rewrite the sentences. Change the adjectives to adverbs.**

1 Mary Rizon is not a good jumper.

<u>Mary Rizon doesn't jump well.</u>

2 Olga Korman is not a graceful dancer.

_____

3 Dana Stoico is not a slow learner.

_____

Put it together!

11 **Who is your favorite sports star? Why is he/she your favorite? Describe him/her and his/her sports style. Write a paragraph in your notebook.**

Example Matt Hadar is my favorite athlete. He can run fast. He's very hardworking and trains every day...

Rewind — Units 3 & 4

1 Fill in the blanks with the superlative form of the adjectives in parentheses.

1 Mont Blanc is _____the highest_____ mountain in Europe.
(high)

2 The Mississippi is _____ river in the United States.
(long)

3 The Pacific is _____ ocean in the world.
(big)

4 The Amazon rain forest is _____ rain forest in South America.
(large)

5 Italy has some of _____ volcanoes in Europe.
(famous)

2 In your notebook, write sentences about the houses in the picture. Use the superlative forms of the adjectives below.

| tall | small | old | new | expensive |

1   2   3

Example   Number 3 is the tallest house on the street.

3 Paul and Susan are talking about the houses above. Fill in the blanks with the comparative or superlative form of the adjectives in parentheses.

PAUL: I like Number 1.

SUSAN: I don't. It's ____the most expensive____ house on the street! I like Number 2.
*(**1** expensive)*

PAUL: But Number 2 is _____ Number 1.
*(**2** small)*

SUSAN: Yes, but it's _____ Number 1.
*(**3** new)*

PAUL: Let's buy Number 3! It's _____ Number 1. It's _____
*(**4** cheap)*   *(**5** big)*

Number 2 and it's _____ house on the street.
*(**6** new)*

4 Write the words in the correct list.

early   fast   funny   late   wonderfully   noisy   quickly   slowly   soft

Adjective	Adverb	Adjective/adverb
noisy	wonderfully	fast

5 Fill in the blanks with the adverb form of the adjectives in the box.

dangerous   easy   good   happy   quiet

1 The children are playing _____happily_____ in the garden.

2 Shh! Talk _____. The baby is sleeping.

3 Tom is a terrible driver. He drives very _____.

4 This isn't a difficult game. Our team is winning _____.

5 Monica sings very _____. She's the best singer in the school.

6 Listen to the rap. Underline the comparatives and circle the superlatives.

I am (the best.) Yes, I am the best!
I'm the highest jumper,
I'm the fastest runner,
I'm the greatest dancer,
I'm the best in the world!

You're not the best. I am the best!
I'm a <u>higher</u> jumper,
I'm a faster runner,
I'm a greater dancer,
I'm better than you!

Oh, come on, guys! Please, stop this now...
We can all jump high.
We can all run fast.
We're all great dancers.
We're as good as you!

We're going to do a project.

(1) 🎧 **Read quickly. Answer the question. Then listen.**

Do the students have an exam this afternoon? — _____

KEN:	Miss Bond, <u>are we going to use</u> the computers today?
MISS BOND:	No, we're not. This morning we're going to do a project. You can do research at the library. This afternoon we're going to watch a video about technology.
HELEN:	Are you going to collect our homework?
MISS BOND:	Yes, Helen. I'm going to correct it tonight.... And tomorrow, class, we're going to use the new computers!
JOE:	Great! Er...Miss Bond, are we going to have a test this week?
MISS BOND:	No, you're not. But you are going to have a test next week!
CLASS:	Oh, Miss Bond!

Got it?

(2) **Read the conversation and 1-5 below. Fill in the "time line" with the correct numbers.**

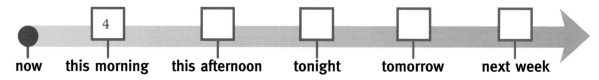

now   this morning   this afternoon   tonight   tomorrow   next week

1 Miss Bond is going to correct the students' homework.
2 The students are going to watch a video.
3 The students are going to have a test.
4 The students are going to visit the library.
5 The students are going to use the new computers.

(3) **Look at the conversation again. Underline the forms of *be + going to* + main verb, as in the example <u>are we going to use</u> in line 1.**

Focus on language!

Future with *be* + *going to*: statements

SUBJECT	+	BE	+	GOING TO	+	MAIN VERB
I		am/'m				
You		are/'re		(not) going to		study.
He/She/It		is/'s				
We		are/'re				
You		are/'re		(not) going to		study.
They		are/'re				

singular — I, You, He/She/It

plural — We, You, They

4 Fill in the blanks. Use *be* + *going to* and the words in parentheses.

1 We _____ are not going to have _____ an exam next week. (*not / have*)

2 I _____ a letter today. (*not / write*)

3 He _____ his lunch this afternoon. (*eat*)

4 They _____ magazines tonight. (*read*)

5 She _____ with us this morning. (*walk*)

6 You _____ to school tomorrow. (*not / drive*)

5 Look at the picture. Fill in the blanks with the correct words.

1 The principal works in the _principal's office_ .

2 The teachers talk in the _____.

3 The students eat lunch in the _____.

4 The students love basketball. They can play it inside in the _____ or outside in the _____.

teachers' lounge

principal's office

cafeteria

gym

playground

Future with *be + going to*: *yes/no* questions

BE + SUBJECT + GOING TO + MAIN VERB				SHORT ANSWERS					
Am	I	going to	study?	Yes,	I	am.	No,	I'm	not.
Is	he/she	going to	study?	Yes,	he/she	is.	No,	he's/she's	not.
	we				we			we're	
Are	they	going to	study?	Yes,	they	are.	No,	they're	not.
	you				you			you're	

6 **Fill in the blanks with the correct form of the verbs in parentheses.**

KEN: ___Are___ you ___going to eat___

(**1** *eat*) at the playground?

JOE: No. I'm going to buy lunch in the cafeteria.

KEN: Oh. _____ Sam _____

(**2** *meet*) you there?

JOE: No. He's in the gym. _____ you

_____ (**3** *eat*) lunch at

the playground?

KEN: Yes. It's a sunny day.... Hey! _____ Helen

and Tammy _____ (**4** *eat*)

in the cafeteria? Umm..._____ you

_____ (**5** *sit*) with them?

JOE: Yes, I am. So..._____ you _____ (**6** *come*) to the cafeteria?

KEN: Umm...OK.

7 **Write questions with the words in parentheses. Then write short answers.**

1 Is he going to study tonight? _____ — Yes, _____he is_____ .
  (*he / study tonight?*)

2 _____ — No, _____ .
  (*they / talk to the principal this afternoon?*)

3 _____ — No, _____ .
  (*you / meet Ken at the playground?*)

4 _____ — Yes, _____ .
  (*we / play basketball in the gym tomorrow?*)

5 _____ — No, _____ .
  (*she / do research at the library tonight?*)

⑧ Today is Monday. Look at Ken's schedule. In your notebook, write sentences about Ken's day.

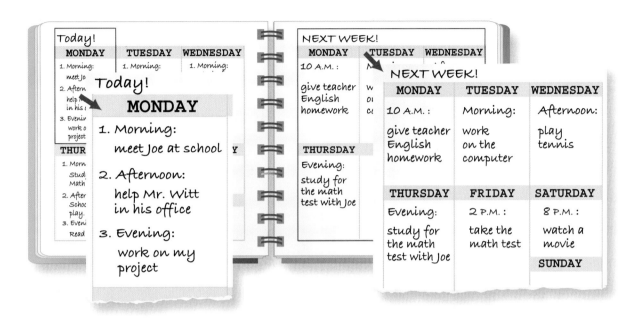

Today!
MONDAY
1. Morning:
   meet Joe at school
2. Afternoon:
   help Mr. Witt
   in his office
3. Evening:
   work on my
   project

NEXT WEEK!

MONDAY	TUESDAY	WEDNESDAY
10 A.M.: give teacher English homework	Morning: work on the computer	Afternoon: play tennis
THURSDAY	FRIDAY	SATURDAY
Evening: study for the math test with Joe	2 P.M.: take the math test	8 P.M.: watch a movie
		SUNDAY

Example This morning Ken is going to meet Joe at school.

⑨ Look at the Tip. Write your sentences from exercise 8 in a different way in your notebook.

Tip
Tomorrow I'm going to see Helen.
I'm going to see Helen **tomorrow**.
Time adverbs can be used both at the beginning and at the end of a sentence.

Example This morning Ken is going to meet Joe at school.

Ken is going to meet Joe at school this morning.

⑩ Now look at Ken's schedule for next week. Write short answers.

1 Is Ken going to work on the computer on Tuesday morning? — Yes, he is.

2 Is Ken going to play tennis on Wednesday afternoon? — _____

3 Is Ken going to watch a movie on Saturday at 8 P.M.? — _____

4 Is Ken going to take a math test on Tuesday at 10 A.M.? — _____

5 Are Ken and Joe going to study for a math test on Wednesday? — _____

Put it together!

⑪ In your notebook, make a schedule of your plans for next week. Use Ken's schedule as a model. Then ask your partner about his or her activities next week.

Example **STUDENT A:** Are you going to watch a movie on Monday?

STUDENT B: No, I'm not. I'm going to play volleyball.

Unit 6

What are you going to do?

1 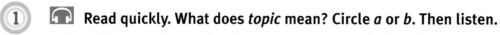 **Read quickly. What does *topic* mean? Circle *a* or *b*. Then listen.**

a Something to talk or write about.   **b** To talk about something.

Homework for May 6th.
Project: "Life in the future."

1 Choose your topic.
   For example: homes, school, transportation.

2 Choose your project.
   For example: drawing, report.

3 Discuss your ideas in groups. Talk to your friends about your ideas.

4 Present your projects in class on Friday.

JOE: This homework is difficult. Let's work together.

KEN: OK. What are you going to do?

JOE: I'm going to draw pictures of cars. I have some cool ideas. My cars are going to have computers, and video games for the passengers.

KEN: Hmm...that's an interesting idea. I don't have a topic. I need help!

JOE: OK, why don't you come to the library tonight? We can choose a topic for you.

KEN: Hey, let's invite Helen and Tammy, too! I'm going to ask them!

Got it?

2 **Read the conversation again. Circle the correct answer. Then fill in the blanks.**

1 The students are going to present their projects ___on Friday___ .

   (**a** on Friday)   **b** after school   **c** today

2 _____ needs help because he doesn't have a topic.

   a Ken   **b** Joe   **c** Helen

3 _____ has some ideas about cars in the future.

   a Ken   **b** Joe   **c** Helen

4 Ken is going to invite _____ to the library.

   a Helen and Tammy   **b** you   **c** the teacher

Focus on language!

Future with *be* + *going to*: information questions

QUESTION WORD	+	BE	+	SUBJECT	+	GOING TO	+	MAIN VERB
What		am		I		going to		see?
Who		are		you		going to		see?
Where		is		he/she		going to		eat?
When		are		we		going to		eat?
Why		are		you		going to		study?
How		are		they		going to		go?

3 **Fill in the blanks with the correct forms of the verbs in parentheses.**

KEN: Hi! I'm going to meet a friend tonight and talk about the homework. Why don't you come with us?

TAMMY: Umm...who ___are___ you ___going to meet___ (**1** *meet*)?

KEN: Joe.

TAMMY: Oh! Cool! What _____ you guys _____ (**2** *do*) for your project?

KEN: Well, I don't have a topic, but Joe's going to draw pictures of cars. What _____ you _____ (**3** *do*), Helen?

HELEN: We're going to write about homes in the future.... Where _____ you _____ (**4** *work*)?

TAMMY: And when _____ Joe _____ (**5** *meet*) you?

KEN: At the library, around 6:30, OK?

4 **Write questions. Use *be* + *going to* and the words in parentheses.**

1 <u>What are you going to read?</u>
 (What / you / read?)

2 _____
 (Who / your father / meet at the airport?)

3 _____
 (Why / they / leave early?)

4 _____
 (When / you / finish your project?)

5 _____
 (Where / your sister / study?)

Future with *be* + *going to*: subject information questions

QUESTION WORD (SUBJECT) +	BE +	GOING TO +	MAIN VERB	
What	is	going to	happen	in class today?
Who	is	going to	study	tonight?

5 Fill in the blanks with *Who* or *What*.

1 __Who__ is going to read this? — Miss Bond.

2 _____ is going to happen tomorrow? — Sam is going to present his project.

3 _____ is going to close at 6 o'clock? — The post office.

4 _____ is going to do research? — The students.

6 Look at the picture. Then match the words with the names.

1 Joe — take notes   4 Helen and Tammy — _____

2 Miss Bond — _____   5 Mr. Witt, principal — _____

3 Ken — _____

7 Fill in the short conversations with the correct words.

> share them   photocopy it   find the books   take notes   borrow it

1 **A:** This information in Al's notebook is very important. Let's _____ take notes _____.

  B: Why don't we _____ ? That's easier!

2 **C:** I can't _____ !... Oh, you have them!

  D: Oh, do you need these books, too? Why don't we _____ ?

3 **E:** We need this book at home tonight.

  F: Why don't we _____ ?

8   Practice the short conversations in exercise 7 with a partner.

9   You're doing a project. Fill in the blanks with the correct verb.

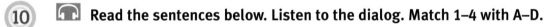

do	choose	present	write

1 First, _____ choose _____ a topic.

2 Next, _____ research on the topic.

3 Then _____ about the topic.

4 Finally, _____ the project.

Tip

Use *First*, *Next* or *Then*, and *Finally* to put things in order in a text.

10   Read the sentences below. Listen to the dialog. Match 1–4 with A–D.

1 First,   A Ken is going to buy ice cream for his friends.

2 Next,   B the friends are going to discuss the girls' topic.

3 Then   C they're going to discuss Joe's topic.

4 Finally,   D they're going to choose a topic for Ken.

Put it together!

11   Work in pairs. First, ask your partner questions about his or her weekend.

Example   **STUDENT A:** What are you going to do this weekend?
          STUDENT B: First, I'm going to sleep late on Saturday morning.
                         Next, I'm going to...

Then write a paragraph about your partner's weekend in your notebook.

Example   First, Tom is going to sleep late on Saturday morning. Next, he's going to...

Units 5&6

1 Look at Jessica's schedule for next week. Write sentences with *be + going to*.

	Mon.	Tue.	Wed.	Thu.	Fri.
morning	meet Sue at the playground	go to the gym	meet Mark for tennis		meet Sarah in the cafeteria
afternoon		take the French test	buy a present for Tony	make a cake for Tony	go to the beach
evening	study for the French test	write a letter		go to Tony's party	go to the concert

1 Jessica is going to study for the French test on Monday evening.

2 _____ on Friday afternoon.

3 _____ on Tuesday evening.

4 _____ on Thursday evening.

5 _____ on Friday morning.

2 Look at Jessica's schedule again. Correct the sentences below in your notebook.

Example Jessica is going to take the French test on Wednesday morning.

Jessica isn't going to take the French test on Wednesday morning.

She's going to take the French test on Tuesday afternoon.

1 Jessica and Mark are going to meet in the cafeteria on Friday morning.
2 Jessica is going to write a letter on Friday afternoon.

3 Unscramble the questions and complete the conversation.

SARAH: Are you going to see that concert on Friday evening?
(**1** going to / on Friday evening / you / Are / see / that concert / ?)

JESSICA: Yes, I am.

SARAH: _____
(**2** Is / going to / the tickets / buy / Tony / for you / ?)

JESSICA: No, he isn't. I'm going to buy the tickets.

SARAH: Hey! Tony's party is on Thursday evening, right?

_____
(**3** for him / Tony's sister / make a cake / going to / Is / ?)

JESSICA: No, she isn't. I am!

4 **Look at Jessica's schedule again. Write the questions.**

1 Who _is Jessica going to meet on Monday_ ?

She's going to meet Sue on Monday.

2 Why _____ on Wednesday afternoon?

Because it's Tony's birthday.

3 Where _____ ?

She's going to go to the beach.

4 What _____ ?

She's going to write a letter.

5 Who _____ ?

She's going to meet Mark for tennis.

5 **Fill in the blanks with the verbs below.**

find	borrow	share	photocopy	take notes

1 Can you _photocopy_ this page for me, please?

2 I'm going to _____ a book from the library.

3 Where is my pencil case? I can't _____ it!

4 Are you hungry? We can _____ my lunch.

5 I always _____ in history class.

6 **Put the pictures in order. Then write Jessica's plans for Thursday. Use *be* + *going to* and the words under the pictures.**

go to a birthday party   buy a cake mix   put on a party dress   make a birthday cake

First, _Jessica is going to buy a cake mix_ .

Next, _____ .

Then _____ .

Finally, _____ .

Unit 7 — Schools will be cool!

1 🎧 **Read quickly. Match the headings and the projects. Then listen.**

a Ken's project on schools in the future ___

b Joe's project on transportation in the future ___

1

Cars will have computers inside. The computers will drive the cars, and they will know all the streets. You won't get lost!

Subways will connect many big cities in the world. We will travel from New York to London under the ground! The subways will be fast, but the tickets will be cheap!

2

Schools in the future will be cool. All students will have computers. Teachers will show students information on the Internet, and people won't carry heavy books! Computers will correct homework, too!

There will be virtual reality in the classroom, and students will "travel" through time and space! In history class, students will "travel" to the virtual past. In biology class, students will "travel" inside virtual human bodies.

Got it?

2 **Read the projects again. Match the beginnings (1–4) and ends (A–D) of the sentences.**

1 Computers will drive cars, and _B_

2 The subways will be fast, but ___

3 There will be virtual reality in the classroom, and ___

4 Teachers will show students information on the Internet, and ___

A the tickets will be cheap!

B they will know all the streets.

C people won't carry heavy books!

D students will "travel" through time and space!

Focus on language!

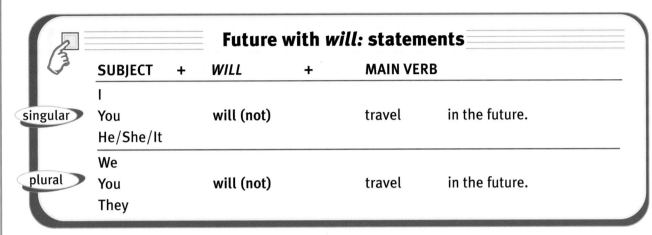

Future with _will_: statements

SUBJECT	+	_WILL_	+	MAIN VERB	
I					
singular — You		will (not)		travel	in the future.
He/She/It					
We					
plural — You		will (not)		travel	in the future.
They					

③ Unscramble the sentences.

1 People will not drive cars.
(cars / not / drive / will / . / People)

2 _____
(have / . / I / will / a / computer / great)

3 _____
(. / be / Subways/ fast / will)

4 _____
(books / We / . / not / carry / will / heavy)

④ Fill in the blanks with _will_ or _won't_.

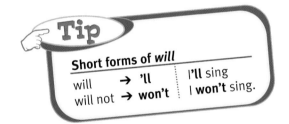

Tip

Short forms of _will_

will → 'll   I'll sing
will not → won't   I won't sing.

TAMMY: Homes in the future (**1**) ___will___ be great!

Housework (**2**) _____ be difficult. Computers

(**3**) _____ clean our homes. They

(**4**) _____ vacuum and mop the floors.

HELEN: Yes! And they (**5**) _____ wash the dishes, too!

People (**6**) _____ do any boring work!

Computers (**7**) _____ do it!

⑤ In your notebook, rewrite the sentences below in the negative form.

Example Computers will do the interesting work.

Computers won't do the interesting work.

1 Our houses will be dirty in the future.
2 People will wash dishes in the future.
3 Life will be difficult in the future.

6 **Look at the words. Then fill in the blanks.**

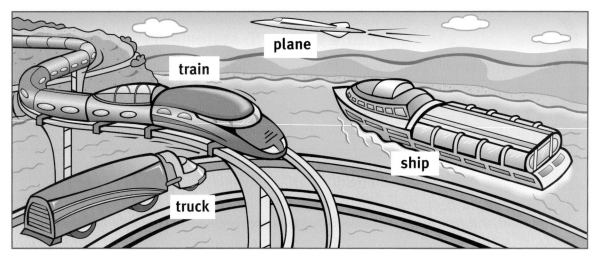

1 It's bigger than a truck. It doesn't travel on water. It's a __train__ .

2 It travels on the street. It's a _____ .

3 It flies. It's a _____ .

4 It travels on water. It's a _____ .

Future with *will*: *yes/no* questions and answers

WILL	+	SUBJECT	+	MAIN VERB	SHORT ANSWERS	
		I			Yes, I will.	No, I won't.
singular Will		you		travel?	Yes, you will.	No, you won't.
		he/she/it			Yes, he/she/it will.	No, he/she/it won't.
		we			Yes, we will.	No, we won't.
plural Will		you		travel?	Yes, you will.	No, you won't.
		they			Yes, they will.	No, they won't.

---

7 **Help Ken answer the questions about transportation in the future.**

1 Will trucks be bigger than trains?   — No, __they won't__ .

2 Will airplanes travel very fast?   — Yes, _____ .

3 Will ships travel on the street?   — No, _____ .

4 Will trains fly?   — No, _____ .

5 Will subways travel around the world?   — Yes, _____ .

8 Read Dr. Dana's predictions about transportation. Do you agree with her? Talk about her predictions with a partner.

TRANSPORTATION IN THE FUTURE

"Scientists will invent new machines for transportation. Press a button, and your car will become an airplane! Press a different button, and your airplane will become a ship or a truck!

Bicycles will be different, too. Computers will control the bicycles. You won't use your hands. In the future, you'll ride a bicycle, read, and eat ice cream!"

Dr. Dana's bicycle of the future

9 Look at Dr. Dana's predictions again. Write *yes/no* questions about the predictions. Then answer the questions. Use short forms with *will* or *won't*.

1 <u>Will scientists invent new transportation machines?</u> — Yes, they will.
   (scientists / invent / new transportation machines?)

2 _____ — _____
   (people / have / cars?)

3 _____ — _____
   (cars / become / airplanes?)

4 _____ — _____
   (computers / control / bicycles?)

5 _____ — _____
   (you / use / your hands on your bicycle?)

Put it together!

10 Work in pairs. Do a project on the future, such as "Cars in the future" or "Movies in the future." Use the projects in exercise 1 as a model. Choose a topic and do research on it. Write two or three paragraphs about your topic, and find or draw pictures. Present your project to the class.

Unit 8

What will you be?

1 🎧 **Read quickly. Circle the best title for Sam's questionnaire and write it on the first line of the magazine page below. Then listen.**

a What will your job be in the future?　　**b** Where will you live in the future?

_____ by Sam Ballard

? What will you do in the future?
Answer the questions below to find out! **!**

1 Are you a good singer?　_____
2 Can you dance?　_____
3 Can you act?　_____

4 Do you love children?　_____
5 Do you love school?　_____
6 Can you explain things well?　_____

7 Do you love planes?　_____
8 Do you love travel?　_____
9 Can you speak two or three languages?　_____

10 Do you like trucks?　_____
11 Can you work alone?　_____
12 Can you work in the daytime or at night?　_____

Central High School Magazine, page 8

Answers to the questionnaire on page 8:

Is your answer YES to 1, 2, and 3? Maybe you will be an entertainer!

Is your answer YES to 4, 5, and 6? Maybe you will be a teacher!

Is your answer YES to 7, 8, and 9? Maybe you will be a flight attendant!

Is your answer YES to 10, 11, and 12? Maybe you will be a truck driver!

Got it?

2 **Complete the questionnaire and read the answers. What will you be in the future?**

3 **Read the answers again. Find the best jobs for the people. Write: E (entertainer), T (teacher), FA (flight attendant), or TD (truck driver).**

1 Eve likes explaining things.　T
2 Ed loves singing and dancing. __

3 Sue loves flying.　__
4 Steve likes driving trucks.　__

Tip

I **like** teach**ing**.
You **love** fly**ing**.

Focus on language!

Future with *will*: information questions

QUESTION WORD	+	*WILL*	+	SUBJECT	+	MAIN VERB
What		will		I		be?
Who		will		you		see?
Where		will		he/she		live?
When		will		we		eat?
Why		will		you		call?
How		will		they		travel?

4 **Unscramble the questions to complete the conversation.**

HELEN: Hey, Ken! <u>What will you be in the future?</u>
(**1** be / What / you / will / future / in / the / ?)

Here, answer these questions in Sam's questionnaire!

KEN: OK! Here are my answers. _____
(**2** be / I / What / ? / will)

HELEN: You'll be a teacher. I'll be a flight attendant!

KEN: Really? _____
(**3** will / Why / ? / you / be / flight attendant / a)

HELEN: Because I love flying!

KEN: But _____
(**4** live/ where / you / ? / will)

_____
(**5** ? / will / you / move there / When)

HELEN: I'll live in Australia. And I'll move there in the year 2010!

5 **Read the conversation again. Fill in the blanks in the questions with *What, Who, Where, When,* or *Why*. Answer the questions.**

1 _____What_____ will Ken be?   —   A teacher.

2 _____ will Helen be?   —   _____

3 _____ will Helen be a flight attendant?   —   _____

4 _____ will Helen live?   —   _____

5 _____ will be a teacher?   —   _____

6 _____ will Helen move to Australia?   —   _____

6 Match the words with the pictures.

A

B

C

D

1 swim → swimmer = <u>A</u>

2 paint → painter = __

3 write → writer = __

4 bake → baker = __

7 Work in pairs. Ask and answer questions using the words in exercise 6.

Example **STUDENT A:** Can you swim?

STUDENT B: Yes, I can.

STUDENT A: Will you be a swimmer in the future?

STUDENT B: Yes, I will. / No, I won't.

Future with *will*: subject information questions

QUESTION WORD (SUBJECT)	+	*WILL*	+	MAIN VERB	
Who		will		be	a teacher?
What		will		happen	to Ken?

8 Read the answers. Write the questions with *What* or *Who* and *will*.

1 <u>Who will be a baker?</u>   — Alice. She makes great cookies.

2 <u>What will happen</u> to Joe? — A man will give him a good job.

3 _____ — Sam. He can swim very fast.

4 _____ to Tammy? — Her teacher will give her a test.

5 _____ — Ken. He can explain things very well.

6 _____ to Lara? — A reporter will write about her.

9   Answer the questions in your notebook. Use *will definitely be*, *will probably be*, or *won't be* in your answers.

Example   Will you be a truck driver?

<u>I will definitely be a truck driver because</u>

<u>I love trucks.</u>

OR   <u>I will probably be a truck driver because</u>

<u>I like trucks.</u>

OR   <u>I won't be a truck driver because I don't</u>

<u>like trucks.</u>

> **Tip**
>
> *Definitely* = 100% certain
> I will *definitely* live in England.
>
> *Probably* = 75% certain
> I will *probably* live in London.
>
> *Maybe* = 50% certain
> *Maybe* I'll live in London.

1 Will you be a hairdresser?
2 Will your friend be a reporter?
3 Will your friend be a vet?

10   Look at the people in the pictures. What will they be in the future? Why? Write your predictions in your notebook. Then, in groups, share your predictions.

Mia

Example   Mia will be a writer because she loves reading books.

Patrick

Sylvia

Put it together!

11   What will you do in the future? Where will you live? Why? Write a paragraph about yourself in your notebook.

Example   I will be a stuntman because I want an exciting job. I will probably live in Hollywood because people make movies there. Maybe I'll be rich.

38

Rewind ——— Units 7 & 8

1 **Fill in the blanks with *will* and the verbs in the box.**

> be   travel   invent   control   have

1 Transportation _____ will be _____ better in the future.

2 Scientists _____ fantastic new airplanes.

3 Computers _____ our cars.

4 Ships _____ on water and on roads.

5 All students _____ computers.

2 **Read about Tommy.**   **Then write about Tommy.**

Today...   **20 years from today...**

1 Tommy cries every day.   **1** Tommy won't cry every day.

2 He doesn't talk.   **2** _____

3 He lives with his parents.   **3** _____

4 He eats baby food.   **4** _____

5 He plays with baby toys.   **5** _____

6 He doesn't play basketball.   **6** _____

3 **Write questions and answers about Tommy's future. Use the words in parentheses.**

1 Will he cry every day? — No, he won't.
    (cry / every day?)

2 _____ — _____
    (his mother / feed him?)

3 _____ — _____
    (play with / baby toys?)

4 _____ — _____
    (play / basketball?)

4 **Match the questions with the answers.**

1 Where will you live in the future?
2 When will we meet in the future?
3 Who will be a writer?
4 What will you be?
5 Where will they work?

A Marcel.
B In a hospital.
C A vet.
D In a big house.
E In eight years.

5 **Write the questions to complete the conversation. Use *What*, *When*, *Where*, and *Why*.**

FATHER: (1) <u>What will Brent be?</u>

MOTHER: Maybe he will be a swimmer.

FATHER: (2) _____

MOTHER: Because he loves water.

FATHER: (3) _____

MOTHER: He'll probably live in Australia near the beach.

FATHER: (4) _____

MOTHER: Maybe he'll go to Australia in 2010.

FATHER: (5) _____

MOTHER: Because he'll finish university in 2009.

6 **Listen to the song and circle the correct words in parentheses.**

Maybe one day I'll be a (1 *star* / *car*).

Maybe I'll be a singer.

Maybe I'll have a (2 *small* / *big*) fast car.

Maybe I'll be a winner!

Maybe one day I'll (3 *drive* / *buy*) a train.

Maybe I'll be a (4 *truck driver* / *teacher*).

Maybe one day I'll fly a (5 *plane* / *train*).

Who can see the future?

Unit 9   There were temples at the Acropolis.

 Read quickly. What does *ancient* mean? Circle the correct answer. Then listen.

a new   **b** old   **c** very old

MELISSA: Wow! Can you believe it, Roy? We're the winners of a big history contest...and we're here in Greece!

ROY: I know! It's great!... Look! The Acropolis! It's beautiful!

MRS. LICATA: And it's very interesting! Why don't you read about it in your history book?

The Acropolis is an ancient wonder. It is on top of a hill in Athens, Greece. It is thousands of years old.

The temples at the Acropolis were very busy thousands of years ago. They are white now, but they were very colorful then. There were also many beautiful friezes and statues in the temples. There are fewer friezes and statues now.

The Parthenon is the biggest temple at the Acropolis. In ancient times, there was a very tall statue of Athena inside the Parthenon. It was about 12 meters tall.

Got it?

 Look at exercise 1. Write *T (True)* or *F (False)*.

1 The temples at the Acropolis were busy. T

2 The temples were colorful. ___

3 There were beautiful friezes and statues. ___

4 The statue of Athena was short. ___

Focus on language!

Simple past with *be*: statements

singular	I	**was** (was not/wasn't)	
	You	**were** (were not/weren't)	in Greece last year.
	He/She/It	**was** (was not/wasn't)	
plural	We		
	You	**were** (were not/weren't)	in Greece last year.
	They		
There	There	**was** (was not/wasn't)	a statue inside the temple.
	There	**were** (were not/weren't)	temples at the Acropolis.

3 Fill in the blanks with *was* or *were*.

1 The temples __were__ colorful.

2 There _____ many statues in Greece in ancient times.

3 There _____ a statue of Athena inside the Parthenon. It _____ 12 meters tall.

4 There _____ friezes in the temples.

5 The Acropolis _____ busy in ancient times.

4 In your notebook, rewrite the sentences in the negative form of the simple past. Use short forms and the words in parentheses.

Example   Melissa and Roy are in Greece this week. (*last week*)

   Melissa and Roy weren't in Greece last week.

1 Mrs. Licata is our teacher this year. (*last year*)

2 There are many restaurants near the Acropolis now. (*three thousand years ago*)

3 Melissa and Roy are sick today. (*yesterday*)

4 You and I are on a trip now. (*two weeks ago*)

5 There are statues in the temple. (*five hundred years ago*)

Tip

Common past time words

yesterday morning/afternoon/evening

last night/week/month/year

five days **ago**

a week/month/year **ago**

5 In your notebook, rewrite the present and past sentences in exercise 4 with *but*. Use a subject pronoun in the second part of the new sentence.

Example   Melissa and Roy are in Greece this week.

   Melissa and Roy weren't in Greece last week.

   Melissa and Roy are in Greece this week, but they weren't in Greece last week.

6 **Fill in the blanks with *was*, *were*, *wasn't*, or *weren't*.**

IANNI: Hi! I'm Ianni! Are you lost? Can I help you?

MRS. LICATA: Well, we're looking for Barbounia, the fish restaurant. I (1) __was__ in Greece ten years ago, and it (2) _____ here then...

IANNI: Oh, the manager is retired now. But his fish (3) _____ as good as the fish at that restaurant across the street. Why don't you go there?

ROY: Good idea!... We're interested in history. Can you tell us about Athens in ancient times?

IANNI: Hmm...well, the temples at the Acropolis (4) _____ colorful.

MELISSA: Yes, but what about life for the ancient Greeks? There (5) _____ lots of parties...right?

IANNI: Well, there (6) _____ parties at people's homes. There (7) _____ dancers, and there (8) _____ great music. But there (9) _____ any stereos, because there (10) _____ any electricity!

7 **Look at the picture of a table in a restaurant. Then fill in the missing letters in A–E, using the words below. (Note: Plural of *knife* = *knives*)**

tablecloth   knife   fork   napkin   spoon

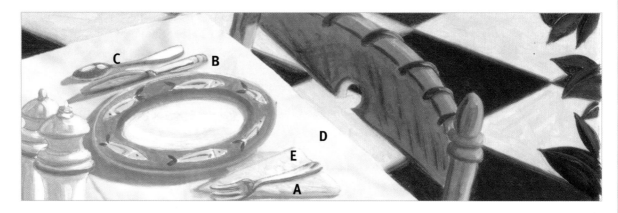

A = f<u>ork</u>_____

B = k_____

C = s_____

D = t_____

E = n_____

8 **Fill in the blanks with the words from exercise 7.**

ROY: This fish is delicious! But I can't pick it up with my (1) _____fork_____!

MELISSA: It's very soft. Use your (2) _____!

IANNI: Would you like some bread, Mrs. Licata? I'll cut it for you. Now, where's my

(3) _____? Oh, here it is.

MRS. LICATA: Thanks, Ianni.... Oh, no! My juice! It's all over the (4) _____,

and it's on my dress!

MELISSA: Don't worry! You can clean it up with this (5) _____.

9 🎧 **Look at the pictures of the ancient and the modern Greek dinner tables. Listen. Circle *T (True)* or *F (False)* for each sentence you hear.**

1 T / Ⓕ   3 T / F   5 T / F
2 T / F   4 T / F   6 T / F

A typical ancient Greek dinner

A typical modern Greek dinner table

10 **Look at the pictures again. In your notebook, write three sentences about the dinner table in ancient Greece and the modern dinner table, using the words below.**

| bread | forks | knives | spoons | jars | glasses |

Example On a typical ancient Greek dinner table, there were probably jars. On a typical modern Greek dinner table, there aren't any jars.

Put it together!

11 **Interview an older person about your town fifty years ago. Ask questions like these:
Was the town big? Were there many people? Were there supermarkets? Compare your town in the past to your town now. Write a paragraph in your notebook.**

Example There was a restaurant next to the theater fifty years ago. Now there is a school next to the theater.

Unit 10

Where were the schools?

1 🎧 **Read quickly. What are the tourists and the tour guide talking about? Circle the correct answer. Then listen.**

a Schools in ancient Greece.   **b** Tour guides.   **c** Mothers.

TOUR GUIDE: ...And that's the Parthenon.

TOURIST 1: Were there stores on the Acropolis?

TOUR GUIDE: No, there weren't. The stores were at the Agora. The Agora was the most important marketplace in the city.

TOURIST 2: What was in the stores at the Agora?

TOUR GUIDE: Well, there was food, and there were animals, too.

TOURIST 1: Where were the schools?

TOUR GUIDE: In many different parts of Athens. But there weren't any schools for girls. There were schools for boys. Girls were at home with their mothers.

IANNI: Look! There's my sister!

MELISSA: Cool! Let's say hi!

Got it?

2 **Read the conversation again. What is Ianni's sister's job?** — _____

3 **Read the conversation again. Match the beginnings (1–4) and ends (A–D) of the sentences.**

1 The Agora wasn't   **A** a marketplace in the city.
2 There weren't   **B** schools for boys.
3 There were   **C** any schools for girls.
4 There was   **D** a temple.

Focus on language!

Simple past with *be*: *yes/no* questions

YES/NO QUESTIONS			SHORT ANSWERS					
Was	I he/she/it	late?	**Yes,**	I he/she/it	**was.**	**No,**	I he/she/it	**wasn't.**
Were	you we they	late?	**Yes,**	you we they	**were.**	**No,**	you we they	**weren't.**
Was	there a store at the Acropolis?		**Yes,** there **was.**			**No,** there **wasn't.**		
Were	there schools?		**Yes,** there **were.**			**No,** there **weren't.**		

4 Fill in the blanks with *was/wasn't* or *were/weren't*.

1 __Was__ the Agora small? — No, it __wasn't__.

2 _____ the tourists in the hotel last night? — Yes, they _____.

3 _____ Ianni's sister with some tourists yesterday? — Yes, she _____.

4 _____ there stereos in ancient Greece? — No, there _____.

5 _____ there animals at the Agora? — Yes, there _____.

6 _____ there girls at ancient Greek schools? — No, there _____.

5 Write questions and short answers. Use the words in parentheses and *was/were* .

1 Were there temples in ancient Greece? — Yes, __there were__.
    (there / temples / in ancient Greece)

2 _____ — No, _____.
    (teenagers / bored / thousands of years ago)

3 _____ — Yes, _____.
    (there / schools / in Greece / thousands of years ago)

4 _____ — Yes, _____.
    (Melissa and Roy / with Ianni / yesterday)

5 _____ — No, _____.
    (she / in Greece / last month)

6 _____ — Yes, _____.
    (there / an Agora / in Athens)

6 Work in pairs. Ask and answer questions about ancient Greece.

Example   **STUDENT A:** Was there a statue of Athena inside the Parthenon?
                 STUDENT B: Yes, there was.

(7) **Fill in the blanks with the present or past forms of the verb *be*.**

IANNI: This (1) __is__ my sister Roula.

She (2) _____ a tour guide. Roula,

these (3) _____ my new

friends...Roy, Melissa, and

Mrs. Licata.

ROULA: Welcome to Greece! Hey...

(4) _____ you on my Acropolis

tour yesterday?

MRS. LICATA: No, we (5) _____. We

(6) _____ at a museum

yesterday.

ROULA: Oh, sorry! Well, how about a tour now? There (7) _____ many statues

in the Parthenon in ancient times, and some of those statues (8) _____

in the Acropolis museum now. Would you like to see them?

ROY: Yes! Thanks, Roula!

Simple past of *be*: information questions

QUESTION WORD	+	*BE*	+	SUBJECT	
Who		was		that man?	
What		was		the boy's name?	
Where		were		you	yesterday?
When		were		you	in Athens?
Why		were		they	late this morning?

---

(8) **Fill in the blanks with question words and *was* or *were*.**

1 _Where_ ___was___ your sister last week? — At the beach.

2 _____ _____ on the phone? — Ianni.

3 _____ _____ you and your friends in New York? — Six months ago.

4 _____ _____ on TV last night? — A documentary about Greece.

5 _____ _____ the statues in ancient times? — In the Parthenon.

6 _____ _____ the ancient Greeks happy? — Because life was good.

9 You are at the museum with Roy and Melissa. Read the sign. Then fill in the blanks with question words and match the questions with the answers.

THE PERSIAN RIDER

This statue is named *The Persian Rider* because the man on the horse is wearing Asian clothes. The statue was in a temple at the Acropolis in ancient times. Twenty years ago, it was in different pieces, and many of the pieces were lost. At that time, the horse's original legs were incomplete. But reconstruction of the statue was an important project for the museum, and now, the horse has four complete legs.

1 ___Who___ was the man on the horse?

2 _____ was the statue named *The Persian Rider*?

3 _____ was *The Persian Rider* in ancient times?

4 _____ was the statue in different pieces?

5 _____ was an important project?

A Reconstruction of the statue.

B A Persian rider.

C Twenty years ago.

D In a temple at the Acropolis.

E Because of the man's Asian clothes.

10 Look at the pictures. Fill in the missing letters in the words. Use plural forms.

In ancient Greece, there were many uses for domesticated animals. For transportation, there were (1) h o r s e s. There was meat from (2) p __ __ __ and (3) __ __ __ __ __ __ __ __. There were clothes from (4) __ __ __ __ __'s wool. And there was milk from (5) __ __ __ __ and (6) __ __ __ __ __.

horse   cow   pig

chicken   sheep   goat

Put it together!

11 Work in pairs. What animals were there in your country one hundred years ago? What were the main uses for these animals? Ask and answer questions about the animals.

Example   **STUDENT A:** Were there horses here one hundred years ago?

STUDENT B: Yes, there were.

STUDENT A: What were the main uses for horses?

STUDENT B: Transportation...

Rewind

Units 9 & 10

1 **Rewrite the sentences in the simple past.**

TODAY   YESTERDAY

1 I am in New York.   _____I was in_____ Chicago.

2 The weather is sunny.   _____ cloudy.

3 There are dancers in the park.   _____ singers in the park.

4 Mom and Dad are happy.   _____ sad.

5 There is a good show on TV.   _____ terrible show on TV.

6 Linda is in France.   _____ in Italy.

2 **Complete the sentences. Use *wasn't* or *weren't* and a past time expression.**

1 Tom is at school today, but _____he wasn't at school yesterday_____.

2 There is a party tonight, but _____there wasn't a party last night_____.

3 My grandparents are in Mexico this week, but _____

last week.

4 It is rainy today, but _____.

5 Rita is at home tonight, but _____.

6 I am busy this month, but _____.

7 We are in 9th grade this year, but _____.

8 You are tired today, but _____.

3 **What do you need in these situations? Match the words and the pictures.**

1 napkin   _C_

2 fork   __

3 spoon   __

4 tablecloth __

5 knife   __

A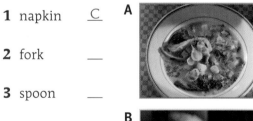

C

E

B

D

4 Fill in the blanks with *Was* or *Were*.

1 ___Was___ Max at a party yesterday?

2 _____ Jenny and Sue at the movie theater yesterday?

3 _____ Mr. and Mrs. Higson in the park yesterday?

4 _____ Trevor in his bedroom yesterday?

5 Look at the pictures. Write answers to the questions in exercise 4.

Jenny and Sue   **Trevor**   **Max**   **Mr. and Mrs. Higson**

1 <u>No, he wasn't.</u> _____   3 _____

2 _____   4 _____

6 Complete the questions with *Who*, *Where*, *When*, or *Why* and *was* or *were*.

1 ___Who___ ___was___ in the library yesterday?   — Max.

2 _____ _____ Trevor in his bedroom?   — Because he was studying.

3 _____ _____ Mr. and Mrs. Higson yesterday?   — At a party.

4 _____ _____ Jenny and Sue at the movie theater?   — Yesterday.

7 Unscramble the letters in the words below and label the correct animals.

| HICNECK | PEHES | WOC | TAGO | SHROE |

1 ___chicken___   2 _____   3 _____

4 _____   5 _____

Unit 11

We fixed the walls.

1 🎧 **Read quickly. What is *reconstruction work*? Circle *a* or *b*. Then listen.**

a Work to fix an old building.   **b** Work to make a new building.

ROULA: Would you like to visit my friend Tasso now? He's an archaeologist.

MRS. LICATA: Oh, yes! Fantastic! I love archaeology!

ROULA: Hi, Tasso. This is my brother Ianni, and these are our new American friends.

TASSO: Hi. Nice to meet you.

MRS. LICATA: Hello! Can you tell us about your work? How often do you discover treasures from ancient Greece? Are you searching for them right now?

TASSO: No, we aren't searching for treasures right now. But we finished some important reconstruction work yesterday.

IANNI: Was the work on the Parthenon?

TASSO: Yes, it was. The Parthenon is very old, and its structure was weak. We fixed some cracks in the walls. And some parts of the Parthenon were in the wrong places. We put them in the right places, but we didn't find the right places for all the parts! My friends are working on the most difficult parts right now!

Got it?

2 **Read the conversation again. Write short answers to the questions.**

1 What is Tasso's job? — <u>Archaeologist.</u>

2 Is Tasso searching for treasures from ancient Greece? — _____

3 Was the Parthenon's structure weak? — _____

4 Were all the parts of the Parthenon in the right places? — _____

Focus on language!

Simple past: spelling of regular verbs

Rule 1   Most verbs: + -ed
          ask → ask**ed**
Rule 2   Verbs ending in -e: + -d
          use → use**d**
Rule 3   Verbs ending in consonant + -y: -y → -i + -ed
          cry → cr**ied**

NOTE: Some verbs are irregular. Examples: win → **won**; see → **saw**; give → **gave**

3 Look at the grammar chart. Fill in the chart with the simple past of the verbs below.

ask	cry	give	watch	move	discover
use	see	win	carry	study	live

Rule 1   _____asked_____   _____   _____

Rule 2   _____used_____   _____   _____

Rule 3   _____cried_____   _____   _____

Irregular   _____won_____   _____   _____

4 Fill in the blanks with the simple past verb forms.

The archaeologists _____finished_____ (**1** *finish*) important reconstruction work.

They _____ (**2** *work*) on the difficult parts for twelve hours yesterday.

Roula, Ianni, Melissa, Roy, and Mrs. Licata _____ (**3** *visit*) them yesterday

afternoon. They _____ (**4** *ask*) the archaeologists many questions, and

they _____ (**5** *watch*) them for two hours. Then the archaeologists

_____ (**6** *move*) some ancient Greek statue pieces to a safe place.

They _____ (**7** *carry*) the statue pieces very carefully.

5 In your notebook, rewrite the sentences below in the simple past.

Example   They fix the cracks in the walls.

              They fixed the cracks in the walls.

1 Mrs. Licata's baby cries at night.
2 The archaeologists work here.
3 The tourists stay at that hotel.
4 We live in Athens.

6 Look at the verbs below. Then fill in the blanks in the chart.

meet	see	tell	take	find
come	have	buy	go	teach

Irregular verbs

present → *past*	*present* → *past*
have → had	_____ → went
_____ → told	_____ → met
_____ → took	_____ → found
_____ → saw	_____ → taught
_____ → came	_____ → bought

7 Fill in the blanks in Mrs. Licata's diary with simple past verb forms.

JUNE 7: We _____went_____ to the Acropolis today. A Greek boy, Ianni,
(1 *go*)

and his sister, Roula, _____ with us. At the Acropolis,
(2 *come*)

we _____ a Greek archaeologist, Tasso. Tasso
(3 *meet*)

_____ us about his work. He _____ us a
(4 *tell*)   (5 *teach*)

lot. Melissa _____ photos. Then we _____
(6 *take*)   (7 *go*)

back to the hotel. Next to the hotel, we _____ a nice shop. It
(8 *see*)

_____ wonderful souvenirs! I _____ some
(9 *have*)   (10 *buy*)

beautiful things! Then we _____ a great restaurant. What
(11 *find*)

a fun day!

Simple past: negative statements

SUBJECT	+	*DID + NOT*	+	MAIN VERB	
I					
You					
He/She		did not/didn't		see	the Parthenon yesterday.
We					
You					
They					

8 **Rewrite the sentences in the negative form.**

1 We saw treasures in the temple.

   We didn't see treasures in the temple.

2 She bought beautiful souvenirs.

   _____

3 They stayed in Athens last month.

   _____

4 Roy and Melissa went to a concert in Greece.

   _____

5 You came home late last night.

   _____

9 **What did Roy do yesterday? Look at his plan for yesterday and correct the sentences about him.**

1 Roy listened to Greek music yesterday.

   Roy didn't listen to Greek music yesterday.

2 Roy found his camera yesterday.

   _____

3 Roy went to the art museum yesterday.

   _____

4 Roy took photos yesterday.

   _____

5 Roy watched a Greek movie yesterday.

   _____

TO DO:
1. see the Parthenon ✓
2. listen to Greek music
3. find my camera
4. go to the art museum
5. talk to Greek people ✓
6. take photos
7. buy souvenirs ✓
8. watch a Greek movie
9. finish my history book
10. tell Mom and Dad about Greece

10 **Look at Roy's plan again. In your notebook, write four more sentences about the other things Roy _did_ and _didn't_ do.**

Put it together!

11 **Look at Mrs. Licata's diary in exercise 7. In your notebook, write a paragraph about what you did yesterday. Include some things you _didn't_ do!**

Example   I woke up early yesterday morning. I didn't watch TV, but I studied for a test...

Unit 12

What did you see in Greece?

1 🎧 **Read quickly. Who are Melissa and Roy talking to? Circle *a* or *b*. Then listen.**

a Officials from a history contest.

b Their friends and families.

MELISSA: Good evening. I'm Melissa, and this is Roy. Thank you for our prize! We learned a lot about ancient Greek history, and we're going to show you some slides from our trip.

ROY: Did we see the Acropolis? Of course! The best thing at the Acropolis was the Parthenon. It was colorful in ancient times, but it's white now! Did you know that interesting fact?

MELISSA: We met archaeologists, and we saw reconstruction work at ancient temples in Greece. It was great!

ROY: And we ate at a Greek restaurant in Plaka, near the Acropolis in Athens! The fish was delicious!

Got it?

2 **Look at exercise 1. Write short answers to the questions.**

1 Did Melissa and Roy learn about history? — <u>Yes, they did.</u>

2 Did they see the Parthenon? — _____

3 Did they go to a Greek restaurant at the Parthenon? — _____

4 Did they eat fish? — _____

Focus on language!

Simple past: *yes/no* questions and short answers

DID + SUBJECT + MAIN VERB		SHORT ANSWERS			
	I		I		I
	you		you		you
Did	he/she **win** the competition?	**Yes,**	he/she **did.**	**No,**	he/she **didn't.**
	we		we		we
	you		you		you
	they		they		they

3 Fill in the blanks to make questions. Use the words in parentheses.

1 _Did you see_ the Pyramids? — Yes, I did.
   (you / see)

2 _____ science on her trip? — No, she didn't.
   (she / study)

3 _____ to a restaurant last Friday? — No, we didn't.
   (you / go)

4 _____ CDs at Bill's house yesterday? — Yes, they did.
   (they / play)

5 _____ his trip to Japan? — Yes, he did.
   (he / like)

4 Use the words in parentheses to make questions.

1 _Did Melissa and Roy go to the Acropolis?_
   (Melissa and Roy / go / to the Acropolis?)

2 _____
   (Roy / see / a Greek movie?)

3 _____
   (Melissa / like / Greek food?)

4 _____
   (Melissa and Roy / listen to / Greek music?)

5 Read the conversation.

ROY: We saw the Acropolis. I loved Greek food, but my friend Melissa didn't like it.

BOB: Did you see any Greek movies?

ANN: And did you like Greek music?

ROY: Well, we didn't see any Greek movies, but we loved Greek music!

Now, ask and answer the questions from exercise 4.

Example   **STUDENT A:** Did Melissa and Roy go to the Acropolis?
              STUDENT B: Yes, they did.

Simple past: information questions

QUESTION WORD	+	*DID*	+	SUBJECT	+	MAIN VERB
Who				I		
What				you		
Where		did		he / she / it		stop?
Why				we		
When				you		
How				they		

(6) **Fill in the blanks with question words and *did*.**

GRACE: (1) __When__ __did__ you come home from Greece, Melissa?

MELISSA: Yesterday.

NEIL: And (2) _____ _____ you do there?

MELISSA: We went to Athens. And we met some nice people.

NEIL: (3) _____ _____ you meet?

MELISSA: We met Ianni and Roula. They're Greek. They took us to a wonderful place!

SETH: (4) _____ _____ they take you?

MELISSA: They took us to an archaeological site near the Parthenon.

We met a Greek archaeologist, and I took photos. We used them

for our slide show.

SETH: (5) _____ _____ you have a slide show?

MELISSA: Because the history contest officials were

interested in our trip!

(7) **Unscramble the words in parentheses to make questions.**

1 Who did Melissa go to the Parthenon with?
(Who / go to the Parthenon with / Melissa)

2 _____
(happen / What / in Athens)

3 _____
(she / Where / meet / the nice people)

4 _____
(from Greece / Melissa / come home / When)

> **Tip**
> **What** happened?
> **Who** called?
> In some information questions, the question word is the subject.

Now answer the questions in your notebook. Use the information in exercise 6.

8 **Match the words with the pictures.**

A    C    E

B    D    F

1 write ➜ wrote   C___   **3** think ➜ thought   ___   **5** read ➜ read   ___

2 eat ➜ ate   ___   **4** wake up ➜ woke up   ___   **6** put ➜ put   ___

9 **Fill in the blanks with the simple past of the verbs in exercise 8.**

Melissa (**1**) __woke up__ very early last Saturday. She (**2**) _____ breakfast at

8 A.M. Then Melissa (**3**) _____ about her friends in Greece. She

(**4**) _____ a letter to Roula and Ianni. She (**5**) _____

the letter in a mailbox. Roula and Ianni were very happy about the letter. They

(**6**) _____ it many times.

10 **Look at exercise 9 again. Write questions about Melissa, Roula, and Ianni in your notebook. Use _Who, What, Where, When_, and _Why_. In pairs, ask and answer.**

Example   STUDENT A: When did Melissa wake up very early?
               STUDENT B: She woke up very early last Saturday.

Put it together!

11 **Work in pairs. Did you take a trip last year? Talk about a real trip or imagine an exciting trip. Interview your partner about his or her trip. Write your questions and answers.**

Example   STUDENT A: Did you go on a trip last year?
               STUDENT B: Yes, I did.
               STUDENT A: Where did you go?
               STUDENT B: I went to Paris. It was great...

Rewind — Units 11 & 12

① **Change the verbs into the simple past and put them in the correct columns.**

like	invent	carry	play	love	cry
have	dance	study	talk	meet	buy

+ -ed	+ -d	-y → -ied	irregular
invented	liked	cried	had
_____	_____	_____	_____
_____	_____	_____	_____

② **Fill in the blanks with the simple past form of the verbs in parentheses.**

I ___saw___ (**1** *see*) a great movie last Friday. The archaeologist in the movie

_____ (**2** *find*) some beautiful treasures. I _____

(**3** *come*) home very late. So, I _____ (**4** *close*) the door quietly and

_____ (**5** *go*) to my bedroom.

I was very tired on Saturday morning, but I _____ (**6** *not / sleep*) late.

I _____ (**7** *wake up*) early. My dad and I _____ (**8** *take*) our cousins to a

soccer game. They _____ (**9** *tell*) me an exciting story. They

_____ (**10** *study*) archaeology at university. One day they

_____ (**11** *discover*) some ancient cups! I _____

(**12** *not / know*) my cousins were so interesting!

③ **Fill in the blanks with the negative form of the underlined verbs.**

1 I <u>finished</u> my English homework, but I ___didn't finish___ my French homework.

2 Ruth <u>had</u> some ham, but she _____ any bread.

3 They <u>played</u> basketball yesterday, but they _____ baseball.

4 Ms. Green <u>taught</u> us about China, but she _____ us about Mexico.

5 We <u>liked</u> the first story, but we _____ the second story.

6 I <u>made</u> the cake, but I _____ the salad.

(4) Carrie and Kim went to Florida on their vacation. Write Carrie's questions, and complete Kim's answers.

CARRIE: I loved Florida.

(1) <u>Did you love Florida?</u>

KIM: Yes, I (2) <u>did</u>.

CARRIE: I went to the beach every day. (3) _____

KIM: No, I (4) _____.

CARRIE: I ate breakfast in my hotel. (5) _____

KIM: Yes, I (6) _____.

CARRIE: I met a famous actor. (7) _____

KIM: No, I (8) _____.

(5) Write Carrie's questions. Use *Where*, *When*, *What*, *Who*, or *Why*.

CARRIE: (1) <u>Where did you go in Florida?</u>

KIM: I went to Orlando.

CARRIE: (2) _____

KIM: Because I love sunny places.

CARRIE: (3) _____

KIM: I went to Orlando on July 3rd.

CARRIE: (4) _____

KIM: We stayed at a big hotel in Orlando.

CARRIE: (5) _____

KIM: My parents traveled with me.

CARRIE: (6) _____

KIM: I saw two studios and a zoo.

(6) 🎧 Listen to the song. Circle all the verbs in the simple past.

Well, I (woke up) this morning.
The sun was in my eyes.
I thought, "Hey, I need some breakfast!"
I ate seven pizza pies.

Yes, I was hungry!
I knew it was true.
I was so hungry, mama!
I wrote this song for you.

Well, it was late in the evening.
The stars were in the sky.
I walked into the kitchen
for one more pizza pie!

Yes, I was hungry!
I knew just what to do.
I was so hungry, mama!
One more pizza?... Maybe two!

Unit 13

He was acting strangely.

1 🎧 **Read quickly. Why is Liza moving? Circle the correct answer. Then listen.**

a Because Liza doesn't like their house.

b Because they're building a new road.

c Because Liza's house doesn't have a yard.

This is my family's last week in this house. We were packing our things yesterday morning. The movers are going to pick them up on Saturday.

I'm very sad. I love this house, but they're building a new road here. After next week, our house won't be here. I know there are traffic problems in this town, but they're building a new electric tram in our area. Why do we need a new road, too?

Speedy was acting very strangely yesterday afternoon! Jeff and I were playing volleyball in the yard. Then Speedy ran out of the yard. He never does that! We saw him under a tree. He was barking loudly.

Got it?

2 **Read Liza's diary again. Match questions 1–4 with answers A–D.**

1 Why won't Liza's house be there after next week? __B_

2 Why are the movers going to come on Saturday? ___

3 Why are they going to build a new road? ___

4 Why did Liza write about Speedy? ___

A Because he was acting strangely.

B Because they are going to build a new road there.

C Because they are going to pick up Liza's family's things.

D Because there are traffic problems in the town.

Focus on language!

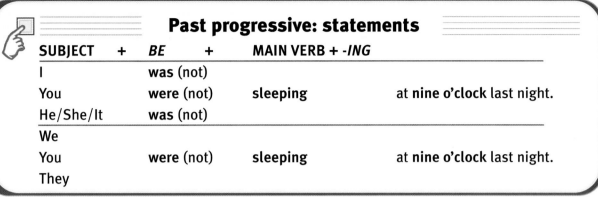

Past progressive: statements

SUBJECT	+	*BE*	+	MAIN VERB + -*ING*	
I		was (not)			
You		were (not)		sleeping	at **nine o'clock** last night.
He/She/It		was (not)			
We					
You		were (not)		sleeping	at **nine o'clock** last night.
They					

3 Fill in the blanks with the past progressive of the verb in parentheses.

Last Saturday at 10 A.M., Jeff and Liza <u>weren't watching</u> TV. They were busy.
(**1** *not / watch*)

They _____ their mother. Jeff _____ the radio,
(**2** *help*) (**3** *fix*)

and Liza _____ . Speedy _____ . Mr. Duarte was
(**4** *vacuum*) (**5** *sleep*)

not at home at the time because he _____ at his office.
(**6** *work*)

4 Look at the picture of the Duartes' kitchen at 8 P.M. last Saturday.
Write affirmative or negative sentences using the words in parentheses.

1 <u>Speedy wasn't sleeping.</u>
(*Speedy / sleep*)

2 _____
(*Liza / water the plants*)

3 _____
(*Mr. Duarte / boil water*)

4 _____
(*Mrs. Duarte / read a magazine*)

5 _____
(*Jeff / drink orange juice*)

(5) **Look at the pictures and the words in the box. Fill in the blanks with the past progressive of the correct verb.**

| push | pull | pack | lock | fall | hold |

1 Mr. Duarte _____was packing_____ some boxes.

2 Mrs. Duarte _____ the car door.

3 Jeff _____ the armchair.

4 Liza _____ the bag.

5 Speedy _____ a ball in his mouth.

6 A box _____ to the floor.

(6) **Speedy was acting strangely yesterday afternoon! Find out what happened. Fill in the blanks with the present progressive of the verbs in parentheses.**

JEFF: Where's Speedy?

LIZA: There! He_'s digging_____ (**1** *dig*) under that tree!

JEFF: Why ___is___ he ____doing____ (**2** *do*) that?

LIZA: Maybe he _____ (**3** *look*) for treasures!

JEFF: That's silly.... Where _____ you

_____ (**4** *go*)?

LIZA: To the tree. Look! He_____ (**5** *hold*)

something in his mouth. What is that?

JEFF: Wait! I_____ (**6** *come*) with you!

(7) **Present progressive or past progressive? Circle the correct verb forms.**

1 Last Sunday at twelve o'clock, we (*are swimming* / *were swimming*) at the beach.

2 She (*is sunbathing* / *was sunbathing*) in the park right now.

3 He (*is holding* / *was holding*) your bag five minutes ago.

4 I (*am playing* / *was playing*) my guitar at seven o'clock last night.

5 The Duartes (*are packing up* / *were packing up*) their things right now.

8 **Read the conversation. Then put sentences A–D in the correct order.**

LIZA: Mom, look at this! What is it?

MRS. DUARTE: I don't know. Where did you find it?

JEFF: We didn't find it! We were playing in the yard, and Speedy found it!

LIZA: Yes! First, Speedy ran out of the yard. Then we watched him. He was digging under that big tree.

JEFF: He dug a big hole! This strange thing was in the hole!

MRS. DUARTE: Well, why don't you show it to your science teacher?

A Speedy found something very strange! —

B Speedy ran out of the yard. —

C Speedy dug a big hole under the tree. —

D Jeff and Liza were playing in the yard with Speedy. 1

9 **Look at the pictures from Sunday. Work in pairs. In your notebook, write a sentence about each picture.**

6:00 A.M.
(*wash / her face*)

6:30 A.M.
(*pack / a box*)

12:30 P.M.
(*pull / an old T-shirt*)

2:00 P.M.
(*dig / a hole*)

2:15 P.M.
(*hold /mouth*)

4:30 P.M.
(*talk /her mom*)

Example Liza was washing her face at 6 A.M.

Put it together!

10 **Look at the times in exercise 9. In your notebook, write the things you were doing yesterday at those times.**

Example At 6 A.M., I was sleeping.

Where were you playing?

1 🎧 **Read quickly. Does Mr. Barr want the new road for the town? Circle the answer in the conversation. Then listen.**

MR. BARR: So...where were you and Liza playing volleyball yesterday afternoon?

JEFF: We were playing in our yard. Then Speedy ran away. We saw him under a tree. He was digging under the tree.

MR. BARR: Was he digging in your yard?

JEFF: No, he wasn't. The tree is in a field behind our house. There was a fence there, but the builders removed it for the new road.

MR. BARR: That's awful! I don't think our town needs that road. People can take the new electric tram to work!

LIZA: So what is this thing, Mr. Barr?

MR. BARR: Hmmm. I'm not sure.... I'm going to call my friend at the museum.

Got it?

2 **What did Speedy find in Unit 13? What do you think? Talk about it in pairs.**

Example I think Speedy found something from an ancient building.

3 **Look at the Tip. Fill in the blanks with *That's awful!* or *That's great!***

1 Liza wants to stay in her house, but she can't. — <u>That's awful!</u>

2 Your brother won a contest! — _____

3 She burned her son's birthday cake. — _____

4 Speedy found something exciting. — _____

> **Tip** 👉
>
> That's awful! ☹
>
> That's great! ☺

Focus on language!

Past progressive: *yes/no* questions and short answers

BE + SUBJECT + MAIN VERB + -ING			SHORT ANSWERS				
Was	I			I	was.	I	wasn't.
Were	you	playing at 3 P.M.?	Yes,	you	were.	No, you	weren't.
Was	he/she			he/she	was	he/she	wasn't
	you			you		you	
Were	we	playing at 3 P.M.?	Yes,	we	were.	No, we	weren't.
	they			they		they	

4 Fill in the blanks to complete the short answers.

1 Were you writing an e-mail at 1:30 P.M.?   — No, _____ I wasn't _____.

2 Was he studying Spanish at ten o'clock last night?   — No, _____.

3 Were your friends gardening at 2:15 P.M. yesterday?   — No, _____.

4 Was she cooking dinner at 9 P.M. yesterday?   — Yes, _____.

5 Were they locking the library at 5:45 P.M. yesterday?   — Yes, _____.

6 Were we driving to the movie at 7 P.M.?   — No, _____.

5 Fill in the blanks with the past progressive form of the verb in parentheses.

1 _____Were_____ you _____sunbathing_____ (*sunbathe*) at 3:00 P.M. yesterday?

2 _____ your cousin _____ (*visit*) you at 8:30 P.M. on Sunday?

3 _____ you and your friends _____ (*watch*) TV at 11 A.M. yesterday?

4 _____ dogs _____ (*bark*) at 1 A.M. last Wednesday?

5 _____ it _____ (*rain*) at 5 A.M. yesterday?

6 _____ you _____ (*vacuum*) at 6 P.M. on Monday?

6 In your notebook, give true answers to the questions in exercise 5.

Example   Were you sunbathing yesterday at 3:00 P.M.?

         _____Yes, I was._____

   OR   _____No, I wasn't._____

Past progressive: information questions

QUESTION WORD +	*BE* (PAST) +	SUBJECT +	MAIN VERB + *-ING*	
Who	was	she	visiting	
What	were	you	doing	at 1 P.M. yesterday?
Where	were	they	going	

(7) **Fill in the blanks.**

DR. LEE: <u> Were </u> they _____<u>playing</u>_____ (**1** *play*)

volleyball in the park at the time of the discovery?

MR. BARR: No. They _____<u>were playing</u>_____ (**2** *play*) in their

yard.

DR. LEE: And the thing was in the dog's mouth... _____

he _____ (**3** *hold*) it, or _____ he

_____ (**4** *eat*) it?

MR. BARR: He _____ (**5** *hold*) it, but he

_____ (**6** *not / eat*) it. It's fine.

DR. LEE: And were the kids careful with the thing?

MR. BARR: Well, let's see.... Liza came into the classroom, and she _____

(**7** *carry*) it in her backpack...

DR. LEE: Oh. Well, why don't you come to the museum after school?... And carry the

thing carefully in a box!

(8) **Read the sentences. Complete the questions and answers using the words in parentheses.**

1 I saw you on Rico Road last night. You were walking fast!

<u>Where were you going last night?</u>   —   <u>I was going to the concert.</u>
      (*Where / you / go*)   (*I / go / to the concert*)

2 We saw them in the park last week. They were playing a game.

_____   —   _____
      (*What / they / play*)   (*They / play / baseball*)

3 I saw her in the cafeteria yesterday. She was talking to a cute boy.

_____   —   _____
      (*Who / she / talk to*)   (*She / talk to / the new student*)

9 Look at the pictures. Fill in the blanks.

purse   wallet   briefcase   watch   backpack

JEFF: Oh, no! I forgot my (1) ___wallet___ .

I don't have any money!

LIZA: I have some money in my

(2) _____ .

It's inside my (3) _____ .

MR. BARR: That's OK. I have money in my

(4) _____ .

Three tickets for the museum, please.

GUARD: I'm sorry, the museum is closed.

MR. BARR: Oh, no! It's 5:30, not 3:30! My (5) _____ isn't working!...

But we're here to visit Dr. Lee!

GUARD: Oh, are you Mr. Barr? OK, you can go in.

10 Read the conversation again. What were they doing at 5:30? Circle *T (True)* or *F (False)*. In your notebook, correct the false sentences.

1 Mr. Barr was looking at his watch.   (T)/ F
2 Jeff was searching for his purse.   T / F
3 Liza was looking in her wallet.   T / F
4 The guard was looking in Mr. Barr's briefcase.   T / F

Put it together!

11 Play charades. Follow the directions and use the following times: *1 P.M. last Saturday*, *4 P.M. last Sunday*, and *7 A.M. today*.

STUDENT A: Ask, "What was I doing at 1 P.M. last Saturday?" Perform the action.

CLASS: Guess what Student A was doing.

What were your friends doing at these times? Write sentences in your notebook.

Rewind

1 Look at the pictures. Fill in the blanks with *was* or *were*.

Yesterday at 9 A.M....

Rover

June and Terry

Fred

Dave and Ann

1 Rover ___was___ jumping in the yard.

2 June and Terry _____ gardening.

3 Fred _____ visiting his friend.

4 Dave and Ann _____ cycling.

2 Write negative sentences. Use the past progressive.

Yesterday at 9 A.M....

1 Rover wasn't eating. _____
    (Rover / eat)

2 _____
    (Dave and Ann / run)

3 _____
    (Fred / call his mother)

4 _____
    (Terry and June / drive to work)

3 Fill in the blanks with the correct form of verbs below. Use the past progressive or the present progressive.

pack	push	fall	hold	lock	pull

1 At eight o'clock last night, I ____was pushing____ my car down the road.

2 Ouch! Mom, Todd _____ my hair!

3 Jenny _____ bags with old clothes right now.

4 Look! The glass _____ off the table!

5 The monkey jumped on Simon because he _____ a banana.

6 He _____ his front door now.

4 **What was the Gordon family doing at 10 P.M. yesterday? Write questions, as in the example.**

1 <u>Was Alan sleeping?</u>
(Alan / sleep)

2 _____
(Minnie and Tibbs / drink water)

3 _____
(Joan / watch TV)

4 _____
(George / make bread)

5 _____
(Mr. and Mrs. Gordon / play computer games)

5 **Fill in the blanks with *Who*, *What*, *When*, *Where*, or *Why* and *was* or *were*.**

1 ____*Where were*____ you sitting at the concert?   — In the front.

2 _____ Tina doing yesterday at 8 P.M.?   — She was taking a shower.

3 _____ driving the car yesterday?   — Gary.

4 _____ you shopping at the mall?   — Yesterday afternoon.

5 _____ the children crying?   — Because they were sad.

6 **Circle the words that don't belong. Then write the mystery sentence with the circled words.**

1 (my)   he   I   she

2 cookie   watch   cake   ice cream

3 buys   buy   bought   is

4 purse   wallet   in   briefcase

5 they   your   we   you

6 backpack   dog   cat   elephant

= My _____ _____ _____

_____ _____.

Unit 15

We were playing when he found it.

OUR TOWN

1 🎧 **Read quickly. Will the Duartes move now? Make a prediction. Then listen.**

HOST: Welcome to *Our Town*! Our guests today are Jeff and Liza Duarte. They were playing in their yard when they discovered an ancient dinosaur bone! This discovery is very important for science. And it will definitely delay the construction of the new road!... So, Jeff and Liza, when did you find the bone?

JEFF: Last week. But we didn't find it. We were playing outside when Speedy, our dog, found it.

HOST: Wow! Were you surprised?

LIZA: Sure! You don't find dinosaur bones every day!

HOST: What did your parents say?

JEFF: Well, we called them while Dr. Lee was looking at the bone, and they were excited. They love dinosaurs!

Got it?

2 **Read the conversation again. Answer the questions. Use short answers.**

1 Did Jeff find the bone? — <u>No, he didn't.</u>

2 Did Speedy find the bone in the house? — _____

3 Was Liza surprised by Speedy's discovery? — _____

4 Did Dr. Lee call Mr. and Mrs. Duarte? — _____

Focus on language!

When / While

I was sleeping **when my friend called.**
My friend called **while I was sleeping.**

Use the simple past with *when*. Use the past progressive with *while*.

3 **Fill in the blanks with *when* or *while*.**

1 Speedy dug a hole _____ while _____ Jeff and Liza were playing.

2 The dog was eating _____ the photographer took his photograph.

3 Dad was watching TV _____ Mom got home.

4 My brother called _____ I was making cookies.

5 The cat took your pen _____ you were reading.

6 My uncle was sitting in the car _____ I went into the store.

4 **Fill in the blanks with the simple past or past progressive of the verbs in parentheses.**

1 My dad came home while we _____ were doing _____ our homework.
  (do)

2 He was watching a video when the little girl _____ him.
  (kiss)

3 My friends arrived while I _____ a shower.
  (take)

4 We were listening to the radio when Mom _____ home.
  (come)

5 I was washing my jeans when I _____ my money.
  (find)

6 She was pouring coffee when we _____ into the room.
  (walk)

5 **Combine the sentences in your notebook. Use the words in parentheses.**

Example   I was sleeping last night. My mom came home. (*when*)

   I was sleeping last night when my mom came home.

1 Marcy was packing her bag. Her aunt called. (*when*)
2 The principal came in. Austin was dancing on the teacher's table. (*while*)
3 I saw a horse on the street outside. I was eating dinner. (*while*)
4 They were riding their bicycles. They saw a beautiful park. (*when*)

6 **Fill in the blanks with the simple past or past progressive of the verbs in parentheses.**

REPORTER: Dr. Lee and Dr. Nunn, what can you tell us about the bone?

DR. NUNN: We _____looked_____ (**1** *look*) at the bone very carefully yesterday. It's the toe of a triceratops dinosaur.

REPORTER: This important discovery will delay the new road construction. ___Did___ you ___talk___ (**2** *talk*) to the mayor about the discovery? _____ you _____ (**3** *discuss*) the new road construction?

DR. LEE: Yes, I _____ (**4** *talk*) to him while Dr. Nunn _____ (**5** *work*) in the lab last night. Then the mayor _____ (**6** *come*) to the lab and _____ (**7** *look*) at the bone while his assistants _____ (**8** *do*) research on the traffic problems in our town. He'll talk about his plans tonight. He'll arrive in fifteen minutes.

7 **Write the words in order from the largest to the smallest forms of transportation.**

| taxi | van | motorcycle | tram |

1 _____tram_____   3 _____

2 _____   4 _____

8 🎧 **Listen to the mayor talk to the reporters. Write *T* (*True*) or *F* (*False*).**

1 The mayor was saying hello when a reporter arrived.   T

2 The mayor was talking about taxis when Speedy barked.   ___

3 People cheered while the mayor was talking about Speedy.   ___

4 A reporter asked about trams while the mayor was talking about buses, vans, and motorcycles.   ___

9 🎧 **Listen to the mayor talking to the reporters again. Circle the correct answer in parentheses.**

1 There are lots of new (taxis / bicycles) on the roads of the town.

2 (Buses and vans / Motorcycles and taxis) travel on roads and carry more people than cars.

3 (Vans / Bicycles) are great for the environment.

4 (Buses / Motorcycles) are smaller than cars and they can travel on small roads.

5 (Trams / Taxis) are quiet and can carry many people.

10 **Write the sentences again using the words in parentheses.**

1 A reporter arrived while the mayor was talking. (when)

The mayor was talking when a reporter arrived.

2 The mayor was discussing the new road when Speedy barked. (while)

_____

3 The mayor saw his friend while he was cycling to work yesterday. (when)

_____

4 The mayor called his wife while the scientists were talking about the discovery. (when)

_____

5 Jeff and Liza were sleeping at home when the mayor went to the lab. (while)

_____

Put it together!

11 **Look at the picture. Read the paragraph.**

It was a sunny day. It was three o'clock in the afternoon. I was walking in the park when I saw a woman. It was Anita Paxton, the movie star! I asked her a question. "Aren't you Anita Paxton, the famous movie star?" She smiled. "No!" she said. "Don't be silly. My name is Lynette!" I was surprised!

Now it's your turn. Paste a photo of yourself in your notebook and write a paragraph about what was happening in the photo.

Unit 16

Speedy is our hero!

1 **Read quickly. Choose the best title for the article. Then listen.**

a Town honors dog hero

b Scientists find dinosaur bones

c Mayor visits museum

The mayor opened a new dinosaur exhibit at the Natural History Museum yesterday. The dinosaur bones in the exhibit were discovered in our town a year ago. Jeff and Liza Duarte were playing in their yard when their dog, Speedy, found an ancient dinosaur toe.

The dog's discovery delayed the construction of a new road. Now, there is no need for the road. When the new electric tram line was opened last year, it was very successful. Many people take the tram to work now, and pollution is not a problem in our town.

Speedy's discovery was good for science and good for the environment. He's the town's hero! The town is going to honor Speedy at a party this afternoon. There will be food, drinks, and a reward for Speedy at the party.

Got it?

2 Read the article again. Where is the information below? Fill in the blanks with *1st* (= first paragraph), *2nd* (= second paragraph), or *3rd* (= third paragraph).

1 There is no need for a new road. 2nd

2 The mayor opened a dinosaur exhibit. ___

3 There will be a party for Speedy this afternoon. ___

Focus on language!

Review: verb tenses

SIMPLE PRESENT:

Use for habitual actions.

I **play** the piano every day.

PRESENT PROGRESSIVE:

Use for actions happening right now.

I **am playing** the piano right now.

SIMPLE PAST:

Use for completed actions.

I **played** the piano last night.

PAST PROGRESSIVE:

Use for ongoing actions in the past.

I **was playing** the piano at 4 P.M. yesterday.

FUTURE:

Use for future actions.

I **will play** the piano at the party next week.

I **am going to** play the piano tomorrow night.

3 Look at the grammar chart. Fill in the blanks with the correct form of the verbs in parentheses.

1 We _____visited_____ the museum yesterday.
(*visit:* simple past)

2 The mayor's assistants _____ the project now.
(*discuss:* present progressive)

3 We usually _____ the electric tram to work.
(*take:* simple present)

4 We _____ Speedy at the party tonight!
(*see:* future with *be + going to*)

5 Famous people _____ to Speedy's party tonight.
(*come:* future with *will*)

6 A photographer took pictures while the mayor _____ to the
(*talk:* past progressive)
reporters.

4 Fill in the blanks with the simple present or simple past of the verbs in parentheses.

1 Speedy _____discovered_____ the dinosaur bone last year.
(*discover*)

2 Mr. Barr's class _____ the museum every year.
(*visit*)

3 Dr. Lee _____ to work every day at 9 A.M.
(*drive*)

4 We _____ the officials ten minutes ago.
(*meet*)

5 Speedy always _____ bones in his mouth.
(*hold*)

6 The reporters _____ in town last night.
(*arrive*)

5 **Fill in the blanks with the present progressive or the past progressive forms of the verbs in parentheses.**

LIZA: The speech _____is starting_____ (**1** *start*) now! Where's Speedy? He

_____was sitting_____ (**2** *sit*) on that chair two minutes ago…. ___Is___

he _____watching_____ (**3** *watch*) the speech with Mom now?

JEFF: No. She_____ (**4** *talk*) to Mr. Barr near the stage.

LIZA: _____ he _____ (**5** *walk*) outside with Dad?

JEFF: No, they _____ (**6** *walk*) outside 20 minutes ago. There's Dad.

He_____ (**7** *drink*) some juice now.

LIZA: Listen! Speedy_____ (**8** *bark*)!

JEFF: Oh, no! He_____ (**9** *jump*) up on the

buffet table! Speedy, no!

6 **Look at the picture. Fill in the blanks.**

1 ___Eggs___ come from chickens.

2 _____ comes

from the ocean.

3 _____ is red, yellow,

and pink.

4 _____ comes from cows.

7 **Read the official's speech. Answer the questions.**

Speedy's wonderful discovery really helped our town. It delayed the new road construction and saved our homes. And now we don't need the road because we have a new electric tram. That's great for the environment! And the tourists love our fantastic new dinosaur exhibit!

It's time to honor our hero, Speedy! I am now going to give Speedy his reward…Speedy? Where are you?… Oh, no! He's eating the steak!

1 Whose discovery delayed the road construction? — ___Speedy's___

2 What is great for the environment? — _____

3 What do the tourists love? — _____

4 What is Speedy doing? — _____

8 Look at the picture in exercise 6. Circle the food that Speedy ate!

9 Fill in the blanks with the simple past or past progressive of the verbs in parentheses.

VICKY: Hi, Liza! How was the party?

LIZA: Hi, Vicky! It was great! But Speedy was very naughty! While the official

_____was talking_____ (**1** *talk*), Speedy _____jumped_____ (**2** *jump*) up

on the buffet table and _____ (**3** *take*) a steak!

VICKY: Oh, no! What _____ (**4** *happen*) next?

LIZA: Well, we _____ (**5** *pull*) Speedy away from

the table when the people _____ (**6** *pick up*)

shrimp and eggs from the table and _____ (**7** *put*) them

on a plate for Speedy! They _____ (**8** *love*)

him!

VICKY: Wow! _____ you _____ (**9** *take*) photos?

LIZA: Yes, I did! I'll show them to you! Speedy was so cute!

He was really excited, and he _____

(**10** *bark*) loudly while the people _____

(**11** *cheer*) for him!

10 Read the conversation again. Match the questions with the answers.

1 Was Speedy naughty?   **A** They put food on a plate for Speedy.
2 Who was pulling Speedy?   **B** Yes, he was.
3 When did Speedy bark loudly?   **C** Jeff and Liza were.
4 What did the people do?   **D** While the people were cheering for him.
5 Will Liza show Vicky photos?   **E** Yes, she will.

Put it together!

11 In your notebook, write about a party you went to. When was it? Where was it? What did you do? What did you eat?

Example I went to a party last week. It was at my best friend's house. We danced and played games. We were listening to pop music when my friend's father arrived. He had a pizza...

Rewind

Units 15 & 16

1 Fill in the blanks with *when* or *while*.

1 Your friend called ___while___ you were sleeping.

2 We were eating breakfast _____ the rain started.

3 _____ I was washing the car, our dog barked at the mail carrier.

4 Stan discovered an old photo _____ he was cleaning his room.

5 Dad was cooking dinner _____ Aunt Mildred arrived.

2 Fill in the blanks with the simple past or past progressive of the verbs in parentheses.

1 My watch _____stopped_____ (*stop*) while I _____was playing_____ (*play*) golf.

2 I _____ (*watch*) TV when Jane _____ (*come*) in.

3 Yesterday, Doris _____ (*wake up*) early in the morning.

4 While she _____ (*sunbathe*), it _____ (*start*) to rain.

5 Grandpa _____ (*wake up*) while I _____
(*vacuum*) the living room.

3 Unscramble the letters and match them with the pictures.

A   B   C   D

1 IAXT   ___taxi___ – _B_   3 MRAT   _____ – __

2 ETOMORCCYL   _____ – __   4 AVN   _____ – __

What transportation is best for each person? Fill in the blanks.

5 **GEORGE:** I like exciting things, and I don't travel with other people. – ___motorcycle___

6 **BRIAN:** I need to move lots of heavy things. – _____

7 **SUSAN:** I want a car to pick me up at my house. – _____

8 **BETTY:** Electric transportation is good for the environment. – _____

79

4 Fill in the blanks with the verbs in parentheses. Use the simple past or the present progressive.

1 She _____is crying_____ (*cry*) because her dog __ate__ (*eat*) her birthday cake.

2 The little boy _____ (*write*) on the wall. Now his father

_____ (*clean*) it.

3 She _____ (*walk*) to work because her bus _____ (*not / come*).

4 They _____ (*go*) to bed at 8 o'clock. Now they _____ (*sleep*).

5 Circle the correct answers and fill in the blanks.

1 Tomorrow, we _____are going to buy_____ a video.
   a bought   **b** were buying   **c** are going to buy

2 Maybe I_____ Japanese next year.
   a 'll study   **b** studied   **c** study

3 Julia _____ her bike to school every day.
   a was riding   **b** rides   **c** is riding

4 We _____ our grandmother yesterday because it was raining.
   a won't visit   **b** aren't visiting   **c** didn't visit

5 It _____ when we arrived in Paris.
   a was snowing   **b** is snowing   **c** is going to snow

6 John can't go now. He _____ me paint my room.
   a helps   **b** helped   **c** is helping

6 🎧 Listen to the song. How many different verb forms can you find? Look at Unit 16 if you need help.

While I was playing my guitar	_____past progressive_____
I met my best friend Susie.	_____
Now we're driving in my car,	_____
We're going to see a movie.	_____
While I was sitting on the wall	_____
I met my best friend Rudy.	_____
Now we're driving to the mall,	_____
We're going to see a movie.	_____

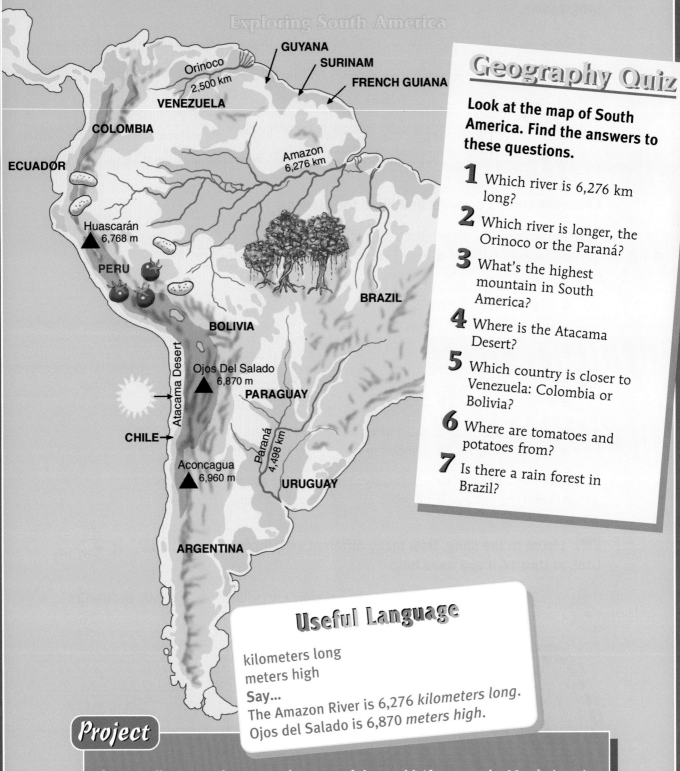

Exploring South America

GUYANA
SURINAM
FRENCH GUIANA
Orinoco
2,500 km
VENEZUELA
COLOMBIA
ECUADOR
Amazon
6,276 km
Huascarán
6,768 m
PERU
BRAZIL
BOLIVIA
Atacama Desert
Ojos Del Salado
6,870 m
PARAGUAY
CHILE
Paraná
4,498 km
Aconcagua
6,960 m
URUGUAY
ARGENTINA

Geography Quiz

Look at the map of South America. Find the answers to these questions.

1 Which river is 6,276 km long?

2 Which river is longer, the Orinoco or the Paraná?

3 What's the highest mountain in South America?

4 Where is the Atacama Desert?

5 Which country is closer to Venezuela: Colombia or Bolivia?

6 Where are tomatoes and potatoes from?

7 Is there a rain forest in Brazil?

Useful Language

kilometers long
meters high

Say...
The Amazon River is 6,276 *kilometers long*.
Ojos del Salado is 6,870 *meters high*.

Project

1 In small groups, choose another area of the world (for example, North America, Africa, or Europe). Draw a map with labels like the one on this page.
2 Write questions about your map.
3 Give your map to another group. Ask the questions.

Transfer to Astronomy

Space Travel

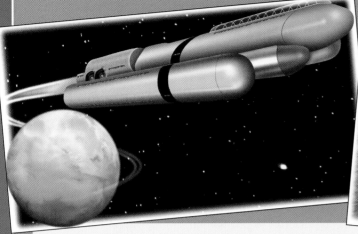

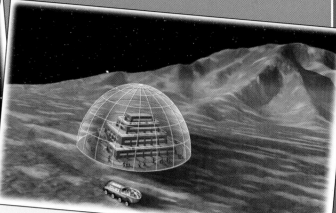

Read the article. Answer the questions in your notebook.

Vacations in Space

Some people think space travel will be a big business in the future. These people are planning a hotel on Mars. They will build the hotel inside a large dome. The atmosphere inside the dome will have oxygen in it. The energy will come from the sun. Tourists will travel outside the hotel in special space buses.

But there are many problems with vacations on Mars. For example, the atmosphere on Mars is 95% carbon dioxide (CO_2). The weather can be very cold. Also, the trip will be about nine months each way. What will people do for nine months in a space ship? Finally, space and the Martian atmosphere are full of dangerous radiation. People will have to wear special clothing almost all of the time.

1 Where will the hotel on Mars be?

2 Where will the energy for the hotel come from?

3 How will tourists travel outside the hotel?

4 Describe two problems with vacations on Mars.

Project

Work in small groups. Imagine that you are a group of business people. You are going to open a hotel on the Moon. Design an ad for your hotel. Do some research to get some information about the Moon. Think about these things:

What is the name of your hotel?
How will people travel to your hotel?
How long will it take people to travel there?
What will tourists do on the Moon?
How much will the trip cost?

Transfer to History

Read about schools in Athens and Sparta. Then answer the questions in your notebook.

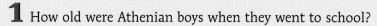

In Athens, Greece, schools were only for boys. Boys went to elementary school from ages 6 to 14. At school, boys learned to read and write and to do math. School materials were very expensive.

For the Athenians, education of both the mind and the body was important. Boys played sports at school, too. They learned to move gracefully, to play ball, and to throw the discus and the javelin. Music was also part of their education. They learned to play the lyre and to sing.

In Athens, girls didn't go to school. They learned to read and write at home. But in Sparta, one of Athens's neighbors, there were schools for girls. In Sparta, education for boys and girls was military and very difficult. For the Spartans, a strong body was the most important thing. The girls lived at their schools from the age of 6 or 7. They learned gymnastics, and they also learned to fight. The Spartans wanted the girls to be strong like the boys. For them, strong women were good mothers.

1 How old were Athenian boys when they went to school?

2 What did the Athenian boys learn at school?

3 Where did girls in Athens learn to read and write?

4 What did girls in Sparta learn at school?

5 How was education in Athens different from education in Sparta?

Project

You can learn history by talking to older people in your community.

1 Work in groups. Write a list of four or five questions to ask about schools in the past. For example, did boys and girls go to the same schools? Were books expensive? (Write your questions in English.)

2 Outside class, ask people in your family, teachers, and other older people your questions. (Use your own language for this.)

3 In class, work with your group. Collect your information and write a report in English for the class. Find or draw some pictures to illustrate your report.

Transfer to Science

What is a *T. Rex*?

Read the article.

In 1902, while Barnum Brown was looking for fossils in the state of Montana, he found some dinosaur bones. The bones came from a *Tyrannosaurus Rex,* the largest meat-eating dinosaur. These bones were the first *T. Rex* bones ever discovered.

The bones are 65 million years old. The *T. Rex* was usually 12.5 meters

long and 4.5 meters tall. It probably weighed over 5 metric

tons when it was living. The *T. Rex* had 60 teeth, and each tooth was 15 centimeters long!

The bones are now at the American Museum of Natural History in New York City. Scientists made a complete skeleton of a *T. Rex* with these bones. They put each bone in the right place. It was like putting together a giant puzzle!

Now complete the chart.

Age of *T. Rex*	
Length of *T. Rex*	
Height of *T. Rex*	4.5 meters
Weight of *T. Rex*	
Number of teeth	
Length of each tooth	15 centimeters

Project

Work in groups. Here are three pictures of bones from a *T. Rex* skeleton. Can you guess what part of the body they came from? Write your answers under the pictures.

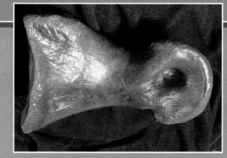

Learning English My Way

Units 1–4
Learn pronunciation from your favorite English songs!

Things to do...

1 Play a favorite English pop song. Listen to the words carefully and look at the words to the song. Memorize the song.

2 Every time you play the song, sing along with it.

3 If you can, record yourself as you sing the song. Listen to your pronunciation. Are you saying the words correctly?

4 Make a list of the words you can't pronounce and practice saying these words to a partner.

Units 5–8
Learn English from movies and TV shows in English.

Things to do...

1 Have a contest. Ask your family or friends to watch a movie or TV show in English. List as many English words from the movie or TV show as you can.

2 Get a bilingual dictionary and check the spelling and the meaning of each word. Correct all wrong words.

3 Compare lists. The person with the longest list of words, spelled correctly, wins.

Units 9–12
English is important!

Things to do...

1 Look for relatives and friends who speak English or who use English in their jobs. Interview these people.

2 Ask "Where and when did you learn English?" "How often did you study English?" "Where and when do you usually use English?"

3 Write a report in English about your interview.

Units 13–16
Set your goals during your vacation.

Things to do...

This vacation, don't stop learning English. Make a weekly or monthly planner. Make entries like:

Week 1	I'll listen to an English pop song and practice saying ten English words.
Week 2	I'll learn five English words from each of the following categories: clothes, food, and furniture.
Week 3	I'll practice some English sentences and phrases with a friend. I'll choose useful English phrases and expressions from my book.

Grammar at a Glance

Adjectives: comparisons

SHORT ADJECTIVES	ADJECTIVE	COMPARATIVE	SUPERLATIVE
Most adjectives: add *-er/-est*	small old	smaller older	the smallest the oldest
Adjectives ending in -e: add *-r/-st*	nice	nicer	the nicest
Adjectives ending in vowel/consonant: double the consonant + *-er/-est*	big fat	**bigger** fatter	the biggest the fattest
Adjectives ending in consonant + -y: *-y → -i + -er / -est*	heavy	heavier	the heaviest
LONG ADJECTIVES			
more / the most + adjective	beautiful colorful	**more** beautiful **more** colorful	the **most** beautiful the **most** colorful

Notes:
1 Comparative phrases often use the word *than*.   Pat's taller **than** Sam.
2 Superlative phrases always begin with *the*.   He's **the** tallest boy in the class.

Adverbs

	ADJECTIVE	ADVERB
Regular: adjective + *-ly*	quiet	quietly
Adjectives ending in -y: *-y → -i + -ly*	happy	happily
Irregular adverbs	good fast hard early late	well fast hard early late

Adjective: Let's take the **early** bus.   She's a **good** player.
Adverb: He always comes **early**.   She plays **well**.

Comparisons with *as...as*

as + adjective + *as*

Sue is as tall as Ed.
I'm **as old as** Carmen.

Irregular adjectives

good	**better**	**best**
bad	**worse**	**worst**

Future: *be + going to* + verb

SUBJECT +	BE +	GOING TO	+ VERB
singular I You He/She/It	am ('m) are ('re) is ('s)	(not) **going to**	dance.
plural We You They	are ('re)	(not) **going to**	dance.

Use *be + going to* for plans.

Future: *will* + verb

SUBJECT	*WILL* +	VERB
singular I You He/She/It	will (won't)	work.
plural We You They	will (won't)	work.

Use *will* for predictions.

Grammar at a Glance

Future: *be + going to (yes/no* questions and short answers)

	BE	SUBJECT	*GOING TO*	VERB		AFFIRMATIVE			NEGATIVE	
singular	Am	I					I	am.		I	'm not.
	Are	you	going to	work?	**Yes,**	you	are.	**No,**	you	're not.
	Is	he/she/it					he/she/it	is.		he/she/it	's not.
plural	Are	we / you / they	going to	work?	**Yes,**	we / you / they	are.	**No,**	we / you / they	're not.

Note: The negative short answers *No, you aren't / No, he isn't* etc. are also possible.

Future: *be + going to* (information questions 1)

	QW	BE	SUBJECT	*GOING TO*	VERB
singular	What	am / are / is	I / you / he/she/it	going to	do?
plural	What	are	we / you / they	going to	do?

Future: *be + going to* (information questions 2)

QW (SUBJECT)	*BE + GOING TO*	VERB
Who	**is going to**	do the work?
What	**is going to**	happen tomorrow?

Note: When the question word is the subject of the question, the question formula is different. The verb in these questions is always in the 3rd person singular.

Yes/no questions

The formula for making *yes/no* questions is the same for almost all questions, in all tenses.

	AUXILIARY	SUBJECT	VERB (+ -*ING*)
1	Do	you	study every day?
2	Did	he	study yesterday?
3	Will	they	study tomorrow?
4	Are	we	studying now?
5	Is	she	going to study tonight?
6	Were	you	studying when I called?

Notice that the short answer usually uses the same auxiliary verb.

SHORT ANSWERS		
1 Yes,	I	do.
2 No,	he	didn't.
3 Yes,	they	will.
4 Yes,	we	are.
5 No,	she	isn't.
6 No,	we	weren't.

Information questions

These questions use the *yes/no* question formula, but they start with the question word.

QW	AUXILIARY	SUBJECT	VERB (+ -*ING*)
What	do	they	do?
Who*	does	she	like?
Why	did	you	read that book?
When	will	we	leave?
Where	am	I	going to stay?
What	was	he	doing at 5 P.M.?

Note: When the question word is the subject of the question, the structure is different.

Examples
Who's in the classroom? (Mary is.)
What happened? (Someone took my book.)
Who will buy the tickets? (Janet will.)

***Whom** is also correct in this case, but it is very formal.

Grammar at a Glance

Simple past: *be*

	SUBJECT	BE
singular	I	was (wasn't)
	You	were (weren't)
	He/she/it	was (wasn't)
plural	We	
	You	were (weren't)
	They	

was not = wasn't
were not = weren't

Simple past: *there + be*

There **was** (**wasn't**) a school.
There **were** (**weren't any**) schools.

Was there a school?	– **Yes**, there **was**. / **No**, there **wasn't**.
Were there any schools?	– **Yes**, there **were**. / **No**, there **weren't**.

Simple past of *be*: *yes/no* questions + short answers

singular	**Was**	I...?		I	**was** (**wasn't**).
	Were	you...?	**Yes** (**No**),	you	**were** (**weren't**).
	Was	he/she/it...?		he/she/it	**was** (**wasn't**).
plural		we...?		we	
	Were	you...?	**Yes** (**No**),	you	**were** (**weren't**).
		they...?		they	

Simple past: regular verbs

AFFIRMATIVE

Add -*ed* to the verb:
I/you/he/she/it   work**ed**.
We/you/they   work**ed**.

NEGATIVE

Put *did not (didn't)* in front of the verb.
I/you/he/she/it   **didn't work**.
We/you/they   **didn't work**.

Simple past: spelling rules

Most verbs: + -*ed*	work	⋯⟩ work**ed**
Consonant + -*y*: -*y* → -*i* + -*ed*	study	⋯⟩ stud**ied**
Vowel + -*y*: + -*ed*	stay	⋯⟩ stay**ed**

These rules are similar to the rules for the comparative and the superlative.

Past progressive: statements

SUBJECT	BE	VERB + -*ING*
I	**was** (not)	
You	**were** (not)	work**ing**.
He/She/It	**was** (not)	
We/You/They	**were** (not)	work**ing**.

Simple past and past progressive: *yes/no* questions and information questions

(See charts in section for Units 5–8.)

When/While

She was eating lunch **when her friend arrived**.
Her friend arrived **while she was eating lunch**.

Use the simple past in *when* clauses.
Use the past progressive in *while* clauses.

1 Complete the sentences with the words in the box.

hairdresser	photographer	reporter	shopkeeper	stuntman	vet

1 A _____photographer_____ takes photographs.

2 A _____ does dangerous things in movies.

3 A _____ helps sick animals.

4 A _____ works with people's hair.

5 A _____ interviews people.

6 A _____ works in a shop.

2 Circle the correct verbs in parentheses.

Peter Walker (1 *is* / *are*) a photographer. He (2 *like* / *likes*) his job very much. Peter
(3 *has* / *have*) a girlfriend. Her name (4 *is* / *are*) Karyna. She and her family
(5 *lives* / *live*) in Hollywood. But Peter (6 *don't live* / *doesn't live*) in Hollywood. So
he (7 *go* / *goes*) to Hollywood every week to see Karyna.

3 Fill in the blanks with *Where*, *When*, or *What*.

1 _Where_ does Peter live? — In Chicago.

2 _____ does Peter's father do? — He's a mail carrier.

3 _____ does Peter's father go to work? — In the morning.

4 _____ does Peter's girlfriend work? — In Hollywood.

4 Complete the sentences with the present progressive of the verbs in the box. Use short
forms when possible.

drive	interview	drink	play	sit

I'm reporter Lucas Mendoza. Today I_'m interviewing_ one of your

(1)

favorite stars. Look! That's Henry Brown, the singer! He

_____ the guitar. The famous actor Tom Shipper

(2)

_____ a big fast car. Who_____ next

(3)   (4)

to Tom?... Hey! It's Lily Wright! She _____ a can of

(5)

soda! This is exciting!

Plus Practice

(1) **Complete the sentences with the opposites of the underlined adjectives.**

1 My city isn't very <u>clean</u>. It's _____dirty_____.

2 The test isn't <u>difficult</u>. It's _____.

3 Big cities aren't <u>quiet</u>. They're _____.

4 Elephants aren't <u>small</u>. They're very _____.

5 These maps aren't <u>new</u>. They're very _____.

(2) **Look at the picture. Correct the sentences about the Big Band.**

THE BIG BAND

Brenda Big
39

Beth Big
17

Barry Big
43

Billy Big
20

1 Brenda is older than Barry.

Brenda _____is younger than_____ Barry.

2 Billy is younger than Beth.

Billy _____ Beth.

3 Beth is fatter than Barry.

Beth _____ Barry.

4 Brenda is taller than Beth.

Brenda _____ Beth.

5 Billy's hair is shorter than Beth's hair.

Billy's hair _____

Beth's hair.

6 Billy is as tall as Beth.

Billy _____ Beth.

(3) **Write comparative sentences with the adjectives in parentheses.**

1 Steve = 70 kilos / Mark = 90 kilos (*heavy*)

Mark is heavier than Steve._____

2 Montevideo = 25° C / Sydney = 30° C (*hot*)

_____

3 The large bicycle = $300 / the small bicycle = $150 (*expensive*)

_____

4 The green book = 200 pages / the blue book = 100 pages (*big*)

_____

5 Jay Jones = *Explore the World* reporter / Bob Jones = my friend (*famous*)

_____

Plus Practice

1 Complete the chart below.

Adjective	Comparative	Superlative
1 interesting	more interesting	the most interesting
2 large	larger	_____
3 beautiful	more beautiful	_____
4 _____	heavier	the heaviest
5 cold	_____	the coldest
6 _____	worse	the worst
7 big	bigger	_____

2 Complete the geography quiz with the words below.

rain forest	island	mountain	ocean	river

1 What's the biggest _____island_____ in the world? — Greenland.

2 What's the longest _____ in the world? — The Nile.

3 What's the highest _____ in the world? — Everest.

4 What's the largest _____ in the world? — The Pacific.

5 What's the most famous _____ in Brazil? — The Amazon.

3 Read the text. Next, answer the questions. Then write the name of each man on the correct line.

Meet Alan, Bob, and Chuck. Alan is older than Chuck. Chuck is older than Bob. Bob and Alan are shorter than Chuck. Alan is stronger than Bob. Bob is as strong as Chuck. Chuck is heavier than Alan. And Alan is heavier than Bob. Chuck is more famous than Alan. Bob is not famous.

_____   _____   _____

1 Who is the oldest? _Alan_   **4** Who is the heaviest? _____

2 Who is the youngest? _____   **5** Who is the strongest? _____

3 Who is the tallest? _____   **6** Who is the most famous? _____

1 Fill in the blanks with the adverb form of the underlined adjectives.

1 The competition is <u>easy</u>. The team is winning _____*easily*_____.

2 Natasha is a <u>graceful</u> dancer. She is dancing _____.

3 That swimmer is <u>slow</u>. He is swimming _____.

4 The soccer team is <u>bad</u>. They are playing _____.

5 The volleyball players are very <u>good</u>. They are playing very _____.

6 The fans are <u>happy</u> and <u>noisy</u>. They are cheering _____ and

_____.

2 Circle the correct words in parentheses to complete the sentences.

TODAY'S OLYMPIC GAMES BULLETIN

Some of the Canadians are (*wonderfully* / *wonderful*) divers.

Some of the Germans are (*slowly* / *slow*) swimmers, but they're strong.

That Russian gymnast is very (*graceful* / *gracefully*).

The Brazilians are playing soccer very (*good* / *well*).

The Americans are playing basketball (*beautiful* / *beautifully*) today.

Those Chinese girls are (*great* / *greatly*) gymnasts.

That Egyptian man always runs (*quick* / *quickly*).

3 Complete the sentences with the words in the box. Then check *Adjective* or *Adverb*.

fast	late	well	early	good

	Adjective	Adverb
1 Karen always arrives ___*late*___ for swimming practice.		✓
2 George Fest is a _____ diver.		
3 Please get up _____ tomorrow. The race is at 7 A.M.		
4 Barry is a very _____ runner. He usually wins his races.		
5 John loves music, but he can't dance very _____.		

Plus Practice

1 Look at the pictures. Fill in the blanks with the words in the box.

| cafeteria | principal's office | playground | classroom |

1 The kids are in the _____classroom_____.

3 Andy is in the _____.

2 The principal and Miss Nash are in the _____.

4 Marla and Lisa are in the _____.

2 Look at exercise 1. Complete the sentences with *be + going to* and the words in the box.

| eat a sandwich | have a test |
| talk about their weekend | talk to the principal |

1 The kids _____ are going to have a test _____.

2 Andy _____.

3 Miss Nash _____.

4 Marla and Lisa _____.

3 Look at exercises 1 and 2. Answer the questions.

1 Are the kids going to correct their homework? — No, they aren't.

2 Is Andy going to eat a sandwich? — _____

3 Is Miss Nash going to play basketball? — _____

4 Are Marla and Lisa going to study for a test? — _____

Plus Practice

1 **Complete the message with the missing letters below.**

a a a a a a a a a a a a̶ e e e e e e e e e e e e e e e e e e i i i i i i o o o o o o o o o o o o o o o o
o o o u

P e t _ r,

D_ r_s_ _rch _n th_ l_br_ry t_n_ght _nd

f_nd th_ b_ _ _k *Th_ Gr_ _ _t C_t*. B_rr_w th_

b_ _ _k t_m_rr_w m_rn_ng. Ph_t_c_py th_ m_p

_n p_g_ 15. D_n't t_k_ n_t_s. M_ _t m_

_n Bl_ck Str_ _ _t _n T_ _ _sd_y _t 11 P.M.

P_tr_ck

2 **Read the complete message again. Fill in the blanks with *be + going to* and the correct verb.**

1 First, Peter _____ is going to find _____ a book in the library.

2 Next, he _____ the book.

3 Then he _____ the map on page 15.

4 Finally, Peter and Patrick _____ on Black Street.

3 **Write the questions. Then match the questions and answers.**

1 Where is Peter going to find the book? _____   **A** On Black Street.
   (Peter / the book / find / going to / is / Where / ?)

2 _____   **B** A map.
   (the name / is / What / ? / of the book)

3 _____   **C** Peter.
   (borrow / Who / going to / ? / the book / is)

4 _____   **D** *The Great Cat.*
   (page 15 / ? / on / is / What)

5 _____   **E** In the library.
   (Where / ? / Peter and Patrick / going to / are / meet)

4 **Why is Peter going to meet Patrick on Black Street? What's your opinion?**

_____

1 Read the paragraph. Fill in the blanks with *will* or *won't* and the correct form of the verb in parentheses.

Life _____ will be _____ easier in the future. People _____ in
　　　　　　(**1** *be*)　　　　　　　　　　　　　　　(**2** *not / work*)

offices. They _____ at home and they _____
　　　　　　　　(**3** *work*)　　　　　　　　　　　　(**4** *use*)

computers to communicate. Students _____ at home. There
　　　　　　　　　　　　　　　　(**5** *study*)

_____ any schools, and vacations _____ longer.
　(**6** *not / be*)　　　　　　　　　　　　　　　(**7** *be*)

2 Look at the pictures. Fill in the sentences with the correct form of transportation.

Cars, trucks, trains, ships, and planes will be better in the future!

1 _____ Trucks _____ will not cause
pollution.

2 _____ will fly in the air.

3 _____ and subways will
be faster.

4 _____ will travel on
land and on water.

5 _____ will travel in
space.

3 Write questions with *will* and the words in parentheses. Then answer the questions with your opinion.

1 Will life be easier?　　　　　　　 —　 Yes, it will. / No, it won't.
　　　　(*life / easier*)

2 _____　 —　_____
　　　　(*we / work at home*)

3 _____　 —　_____
　　　　(*students / study at home*)

4 _____　 —　_____
　　　　(*there be / schools*)

5 _____　 —　_____
　　　　(*transportation / be better*)

6 _____　 —　_____
　　　　(*cars / fly*)

1 Complete the chart. Then use some of the occupations to complete the sentences.

VERB	⟶	OCCUPATION
bake	⟶	baker
entertain	⟶	_____
paint	⟶	_____
report	⟶	_____
write	⟶	_____
teach	⟶	_____

1 Karen makes delicious cakes. She'll probably be a _____ baker _____.

2 Michael writes wonderful stories. He'll definitely be a _____.

3 Pablo's paintings are so beautiful! He'll definitely be a _____.

4 Mabel loves the news. She'll probably be a _____.

5 Veronica can play the piano very well. She'll probably be an _____.

2 Write the teacher's questions. Use question words and *will*.

TEACHER: (1) _____ What will _____ you do in the future?

SARAH: I'll be a teacher.

TEACHER: (2) _____

SARAH: Because I love books and children.

TEACHER: (3) _____

SARAH: I'll probably work in a big school.

TEACHER: (4) _____

SARAH: I'll start work after I finish university.

3 Circle the correct answers.

1 Are you a good driver?
  a Yes, you are.   **b** No, they aren't.   **c** Yes, I am.

2 Are they going to play golf tomorrow?
  a Yes, they do.   **b** No, they aren't.   **c** No, we aren't.

3 Do you like traveling?
  a Yes, I will.   **b** No, I won't.   **c** Yes, I like it.

4 Can you play the piano?
  a Yes, I can.   **b** No, they can't.   **c** Yes, I do.

5 Will Alicia live in Mexico?
  a Yes, she will.   **b** No, she isn't.   **c** Yes, he will.

Plus Practice

1 Look at the list of inventions below. Then complete the sentences with *There was* or *There wasn't, There were* or *There weren't*.

INVENTIONS	YEAR
1 Automobile	1885
2 Telephone	1876
3 Electricity	1881
4 Television	1926
5 Personal computer	1974

1 _____There weren't_____ any automobiles two hundred years ago.

2 _____ telephones one hundred years ago.

3 _____ any electricity one hundred and fifty years ago.

4 _____ television sixty years ago.

5 _____ any personal computers fifty years ago.

2 Read the postcard. Fill in the blanks with *was* or *were*.

October 12th

Dear Anne,

   England is a fantastic country! I love the people, the cities, and the museums.

I ___was___ in London last week. There _____ many tourists and
  (1)   (2)

the hotels _____ very expensive!
           (3)

   I visited many interesting places in London. I _____ in Kew Gardens
                                                    (4)

last Saturday. On Sunday, I _____ at a museum. There _____
                            (5)   (6)

many interesting antiques there. The forks, knives, and spoons _____
                                                                (7)

the most beautiful antiques. They were hundreds of years old!

Love, Tessa

Anne Smith

12B Oliver Dr.

San Diego, CA

USA

3 Read the postcard again. Circle the correct answer.

1 Tessa (*doesn't like England /* (likes England)).

2 Anne (*lives in England / lives in the United States*).

3 The hotels in London were (*fantastic / expensive*).

4 Last Saturday Tessa was (*in Kew Gardens / at a museum*).

Plus Practice

1 Write the names of the objects or animals under the pictures.

1 ____fork____   **3** _____   **5** _____   **7** _____

2 _____   **4** _____   **6** _____   **8** _____

2 Write the words in exercise 1 on the right lines.

    1 Animals   = ____horse,_____

    2 Things on a table = ____fork,_____

3 Complete the questions with the words in parentheses and *was* or *wasn't*, *were* or *weren't*. Then, answer the questions.

    1 Was Rome a very important city thousands of years ago? _____

                 (*Rome / a very important city thousands of years ago*)

      Yes, it ____was____.

    2 _____

               (*Winston Churchill and Mahatma Gandhi / famous men*)

      Yes, they _____.

    3 _____

               (*Albert Einstein / an archaeologist*)

      No, he _____. He was a great scientist.

    4 _____

               (*John F. Kennedy and Abraham Lincoln / entertainers*)

      No, they _____. They were presidents of the United States.

4 Complete the questions with *Who*, *Where*, *What*, or *When* and *was* or *were*.

    1 __Who__ ____was____ Shakespeare?   — A famous English writer.

    2 _____ _____ *Titanic*?   — A movie.

    3 _____ _____ Plato and Aristotle from? — Ancient Greece.

    4 _____ _____ the first trip to the moon? — In 1969.

    5 _____ _____ Picasso and van Gogh? — Famous painters.

1 Look at the pictures. Joe did many things on Saturday. Write sentences with the phrases in the box and the simple past of the verbs.

| listen to music | visit a friend | study for a test |
| play tennis | use the computer | talk on the phone |

1 <u>He studied for a test.</u>

4 _____

2 _____

5 _____

3 _____

6 _____

2 Fill in the blanks with the correct form of the verbs below.

| go | find | make | stay | tell |

1 Joe's brother _____ told _____ Joe, but he didn't _____ tell _____ his sisters.

2 Joe's sisters _____ to the shopping mall, but they didn't

_____ to the movies.

3 Joe's parents _____ at home, but they didn't

_____ in the yard.

4 Joe's grandmother _____ a cake, but she didn't

_____ cookies.

5 Joe's mother _____ Joe's socks under the bed, but she didn't

_____ his shoes.

1 **Read the page from Jane's diary. Then answer the questions.**

Yesterday was Saturday. I love Saturdays because I can wake up late! I woke up at 10:00, ate my breakfast, and read the newspaper. Then I wrote an e-mail to my friend John. In the afternoon, I went to the park and met my friends Gina and Paul. I had a wonderful day.

1 Did Jane go to a park yesterday? — <u>Yes, she did.</u>

2 Did Jane go to school yesterday? — _____

3 Did Gina and Paul meet Jane yesterday? — _____

4 Did Jane wake up at 7 A.M. yesterday? — _____

5 Did Jane read the newspaper yesterday? — _____

6 Did Jane write an e-mail yesterday? — _____

2 **Write questions with the words in parentheses. Use the simple past.**

1 <u>What time did Jane wake up yesterday morning?</u> _____
   (What time / Jane / wake up / yesterday morning)

2 _____
   (What / Jane / do / yesterday afternoon)

3 _____
   (Who / Jane / see / an hour ago)

4 _____
   (Where / Jane's parents / go / last weekend)

5 _____
   (When / Jane's cousin / move)

6 _____
   (Why / Paul / buy a present / last Tuesday)

3 **Match the answers below to the questions in exercise 2.**

<u>6</u> **A** Because it was Gina's birthday.   ___ **D** She went to Gina's party.

___ **B** To the theater.   ___ **E** On Saturday.

___ **C** At 10 A.M.   ___ **F** Paul.

1 It is 8 P.M. What are the people on Liza's street doing? Complete the sentences. Use the present progressive and the words in parentheses.

1 The Andersons _____ are watching a video _____ .
(watch / a video)

2 Jack Taylor _____ .
(play / the piano)

3 The Stevens _____ .
(eat / dinner)

4 Liza Monello _____ .
(vacuum / the floor)

2 An hour ago, the people on Liza's street were doing different things. Fill in the blanks with the past progressive of the verbs in parentheses.

At 7 P.M., the Andersons _____ were not watching _____ TV. They _____ were cooking _____
(**1** not / watch) (**2** cook)

dinner. Jack Taylor _____ the piano. He _____
(**3** not / play) (**4** walk)

home. The Stevens _____ dinner. They _____
(**5** not / eat) (**6** buy)

food at the supermarket. Liza Monello _____ the floor. She
(**7** not / vacuum)

_____ some coffee.
(**8** drink)

3 Fill in the blanks with the past progressive of the verbs below.

| fall hold lock pack pull push walk |

1 Last Sunday at 8:05 Laura _____ was packing _____ her bag and Fred

_____ was pushing _____ the door open.

2 At 8:06, Laura _____ the bag with a key and

Fred _____ into the room. He _____

an ice cream.

3 At 8:07, Laura _____ her bag up and Fred's ice cream

_____ on the floor.

Plus Practice

1 **Write the questions with the words in parentheses. Use the past progressive.**

MRS. RILEY: It's 10:30! You're late... Oh! What

happened to you?

MARK: I fell.

MRS. RILEY: <u>What were you doing?</u>
       (1 *What / you / do?)*

MARK: I was playing basketball.

MRS. RILEY: _____
                    (2 *Who / play with you?)*

MARK: Fred and Leo.

MRS. RILEY: _____
                    (3 *Where / you / play?)*

MARK: In the gym.

MRS. RILEY: But you don't have gym class today. _____
                                                  (4 *Why / you / play?)*

MARK: Because Mr. Carter was sick today, so we went to the gym.

2 **Look at the conversation. Answer the questions.**

1 Was Mark studying at nine o'clock this morning?   — <u>No, he wasn't.</u>

2 Were Fred and Leo playing basketball this morning?   — _____

3 Were the boys playing in the park this morning?   — _____

4 Was Mr. Carter teaching this morning?   — _____

5 Was Mark talking to Mrs. Riley at 10:30 this morning?   — _____

3 **What are the objects below? Fill in the blanks and complete the words.**

1 Women use this more than men.   p <u>u</u> <u>r</u> <u>s</u> <u>e</u>

2 You can carry your books in it.   b __ __ __ __ __ __ __

3 You can carry papers in it.   b __ __ __ __ __ __

4 You can carry money in it.   w __ __ __ __ __

5 You can see the time on it.   w __ __ __ __

Plus Practice

Unit 15

(1) **Paul, Tim, Claudia, and Richie were at the club yesterday. Circle the correct form of the verbs in parentheses.**

Tim and Paul (**1** ⟨*were playing*⟩ / *played*) tennis when the rain (**2** *was starting* / *started*). While they (**3** *were running* / *ran*) back to the club, they (**4** *were seeing* / *saw*) Claudia and Richie in the garden. Claudia (**5** *was teaching* / *taught*) Richie mini-golf, and they (**6** *were having* / *had*) fun. But the club manager (**7** *was telling* / *told*) them to come inside. While they (**8** *were looking* / *looked*) for their golf balls, Paul (**9** *was making* / *made*) hot coffee for them.

(2) **Fill in the blanks with the simple past or past progressive of the verbs in parentheses.**

1 The students _____were working_____ (*work*) in the library when they

_____finished_____ (*finish*) their science project yesterday.

2 A horse _____ (*walk*) out on the field while the Rocket soccer team

_____ (*play*) last Sunday.

3 Scientists were working on dinosaur research in the United States when archaeologists

_____ (*discover*) dinosaur bones in Africa last year.

4 Many people watched TV while the reporters _____ (*interview*) the

children.

(3) **Complete the word groups with the correct words from the box.**

classroom	island	photographer	soft	van

1 cafeteria, gym, playground, _____classroom_____

2 river, ocean, mountain, _____

3 taxi, motorcycle, tram, _____

4 shopkeeper, hairdresser, mail carrier, _____

5 dirty, noisy, sunny, _____

103

1 Complete the sentences with the simple present or simple past of the verbs in parentheses.

1 John and his friends _____*went*_____ to the movies yesterday.
(*go*)

2 We _____ fish for dinner last Sunday.
(*eat*)

3 We always _____ on our summer vacations.
(*travel*)

4 Helen _____ to go to the theater on Saturday nights.
(*love*)

5 I _____ late last Monday.
(*wake up*)

2 Circle the correct form of the verbs in parentheses.

1 Janet (*was writing* / *is writing*) an e-mail when I saw her in the living room.
2 Nathan (*is finding* / *found*) many eggs in the chicken house yesterday.
3 Marina and Bruno (*were visiting* / *will visit*) their friends in Rome next summer.
4 My friends and I (*were dancing* / *are dancing*) when they stopped the music.

3 Circle the correct verb forms and complete the sentences.

1 She was running in the park when she _____ Jerry.

  a met   **b** meet   **c** was meeting

2 The students _____ their homework when the teacher arrived.

  a are doing   **b** were doing   **c** did

3 They came home while I _____ steaks yesterday.

  a cook   **b** was cooking   **c** didn't cook

4 My sister _____ me an hour ago.

  a called   **b** calls   **c** is going to call

4 You're having a party! Label the pictures. Then choose two foods for your party.

1 ____*shrimp*____   3 _____   5 _____

2 _____   4 _____   6 _____

Wordmaster

This list shows the new key words in this book and where they are introduced. Use the list to practice them. Draw pictures or write sentences with the words. Or write a definition.

Aa

act **8**-1 _____

action **1**-1 _____

after **6**-2 _____

ago **9**T _____

airport **6**-4 _____

alone **8**-1 _____

anaconda **3**-8 _____

ancient **9**-1 _____

archaeological **12**-6 _____

archaeologist **11**-1 _____

archaeology **11**-1 _____

area **13**-1 _____

arrive **15**-6 _____

art **11**-9 _____

as...as **2**-1 _____

Asian **10**-9 _____

ask **6**-1 _____

away **14**-1 _____

awful **14**-1 = terrible _____

Bb

back **11**-7 _____

backpack **14**-7 _____

bake **8**-6 _____

baker **8**-6 _____

bark **13**-1 _____

beach **3**-1 _____

beautifully **4**-4 _____

become **7**-8 _____

below **8**-1 _____

best **3**-8 _____

better **3**T _____

biology **7**-1 _____

body **7**-1 _____

bone **15**-1 _____

bored **10**-5 _____

borrow **6**-6 _____

briefcase **14**-9 _____

buffet **16**-5 _____

build **13**-1 _____

builder **14**-1 _____

button **7**-8 _____

buy **5**-6 _____

by **15**-2 _____

Cc

cafeteria **5**-5 _____

carefully **11**-4 _____

carry **7**-1 _____

cash register **1**-8 _____

certain **8**T _____

cheap **2**-1 _____

cheer **4**-1 _____

chicken **10**-10 _____

Chinese **4**-3 _____

choose **6**-1 _____

climber **3**-1 _____

close **6**-5 _____

closed **14**-9 _____

collect **2**-1 _____

colorful **2**-1 _____

compete **4**-1 _____

concert hall **2**-7 _____

connect **7**-1 _____

construction **15**-1 _____

control **7**-9 _____

correct **5**-1 _____

cow **10**-10 _____

crack **11**-1 _____

Wordmaster

Dd

dancer **4**-8 _____

daytime **8**-1 _____

definitely **8**-9 _____

delay **15**-1 _____

dig **13**-6 _____

dinosaur **15**-1 _____

dirty **2**-6 _____

discover **11**-1 _____

discovery **14**-7 _____

discuss **6**-1 _____

diver **4**-6 _____

domesticated **10**-10 _____

door **13**-5 _____

down **3**-4 _____

Ee

early **4**-5 _____

earth **3**-4 _____

easier **6**-7 _____

easily **4**-1 _____

easy **1**-4 _____

egg **16**-6 _____

electric **13**-1 _____

elephant **2**-1 _____

end **3**-4 _____

entertainer **8**-1 _____

everyone **3**-1 _____

excited **15**-1 _____

exhibit **16**-1 _____

expensive **2**-1 _____

explain **8**-1 _____

explore **1**-1 _____

Ff

fact **12**-1 _____

fall **13**-5 _____

famous **2**-8 _____

fast **4**-5 _____

fat **2**-1 _____

fence **14**-1 _____

fewer **9**-1 _____

field **14**-1 _____

finally **6**T _____

find **6**-6 _____

fish **9**-6 _____

flight attendant **8**-1 _____

forget **14**-9 _____

fork **9**-7 _____

friendliest **3**-1 _____

frieze **9**-1 _____

fruit salad **16**-6 _____

future **6**-1 _____

Gg

goat **10**-10 _____

graceful **4**-7 _____

gracefully **4**-6 The gymnast jumped gracefully.

Greek **9**-6 _____

ground **7**-1 _____

guard **14**-9 _____

guest **15**-1 _____

guide **3**-1 _____

gym **5**-5 _____

gymnast **4**-6 _____

Hh

hairdresser **1**-8 _____

happily **4**-4 _____

hard **2**-6 _____

hero **16**-1 _____

highest **3**-1 _____

hill **9**-1 _____

history **1**-5 _____

hold **13**-5 _____

hole **13**-8 _____

home **4**-1 _____

honor **16**-1 _____

horse **10**-9 _____

horseman **10**-9 _____

hotel **10**-4 _____

housework **7**-4 _____

human **7**-1 _____

Ii

important **3**-6 _____

Wordmaster

incomplete **10**-9 _____

incredible **3**-1 _____

Indian **2**-8 _____

information **6**-7 _____

inside **7**-1 _____

interested **9**-6 _____

interesting **2**-1 _____

international **1**-1 _____

Internet **7**-1 _____

interview **1**-3 _____

invent **7**-8 _____

invite **6**-1 _____

island **3**-5 _____

Jj

jeans **15**-4 _____

jumper **4**-8 _____

junk **2**-1 _____

Kk

Kenyan **1**-1 _____

knife **9**-7 _____

Ll

last **9**T _____

later **3**-1 _____

learner **4**-10 _____

life **7**-5 _____

lion cub **1**-1 _= a baby lion_ _____

lock **13**-5 _____

lost **7**-1 _____

lots **9**-6 _____

loudly **13**-1 _____

Mm

mail carrier **1**-8 _____

mail bag **1**-8 _____

mailbox **12**-9 _____

manager **9**-6 _____

marketplace **10**-1 _____

meat **10**-10 _____

meet **5**-6 _____

meter **9**-1 _____

Mexican **4**-3 _____

more **2**-1 _____

most **3**-1 _____

motorcycle **15**-7 _____

mountain **3**-1 _____

move **8**-4 _____

mover **13**-1 _____

museum **10**-7 _____

Nn

napkin **9**-7 _____

need **6**-1 _____

noisily **4**-1 _____

noisy **2**-6 _____

Oo

ocean **3**-5 _____

of course! **12**-1 _____

official **12**-1 _____

Olympic Games **4**-1 _____

Olympic Village **4**-1 _____

only **2**-1 _____

open **16**-1 _____

original **10**-9 _____

other **3**-4 _____

out **8**-1 _____

Pp

pack **13**-1 _____

painter **8**-6 _____

part **11**-1 _____

passenger **6**-1 _____

past **7**-1 _____

perform **4**-3 _____

Persian **10**-9 _____

photocopy **6**-6 _____

photographer **1**-8 _____

pick up **9**-8 _____

piece **10**-9 _____

pig **10**-10 _____

Wordmaster

plan **15**-6 _____

plane **7**-6 _____

playground **5**-5 _____

present **6**-1 _____

press **7**-8 _____

principal's office **5**-5 _____

probably **8**-9 _____

project **5**-1 _____

pull **13**-5 _____

purse **14**-9 _____

push **13**-5 _____

pyramid **3**-4 _____

python **3**-8 _____

Qq

questionnaire **8**-1 _____

quickly **4**-6 _____

quietly **4**-1 _____

Rr

race **4**-4 _____

rain forest **3**-5 _____

reconstruction **1**-9 _____

remove **14**-1 _____

report **1**-1 _____

reporter **1**-1 _____

research **5**-1 _____

retired **9**-6 _____

reward **16**-1 _____

ride **7**-8 _____

rider **10**-9 _____

river **3**-5 _____

runner **4**-4 _____

Russian **4**-5 _____

Ss

safe **11**-4 _____

save **16**-7 _____

scissors **1**-8 _____

scorer **4**-9 _____

search **11**-1 _____

sell **1**-9 _____

sheep **10**-10 _____

ship **7**-6 _____

shop **4**-1 _____

shopkeeper **1**-8 _____

shrimp **16**-6 _____

sick **1**-1 _____

site **12**-6 _____

slide **12**-1 _____

slide show **12**-6 _____

slow **4**-7 _____

slowly **4**-6 _____

smile **4**-4 _____

snake **3**-8 _____

soft **2**-6 _____

souvenir **11**-7 _____

space **7**-1 _____

speech **16**-5 _____

spoon **9**-7 ___You eat soup with a spoon.___

stadium **4**-5 _____

stage **16**-5 _____

statue **2**-1 _____

steak **16**-6 _____

strange **13**-8 _____

strangely **13**-1 _____

structure **11**-1 _____

stunt **1**-4 _____

stuntman **1**-1 _____

subway **7**-1 _____

successful **16**-1 _____

surprised **15**-1 _____

swimmer **8**-6 _____

Tt

tablecloth **9**-7 _____

take notes **6**-6 _____

taxi **15**-7 _____

teachers' lounge **5**-5 _____

technology **5**-1 _____

teen/teenager **1**-1 _____

temple **9**-1 _____

than **2**-1 _____

then **6**T _____

Wordmaster

through **7**-1 _____

together **6**-1 _____

tomorrow **5**-1 _____

tonight **2**-8 _____

topic **6**-1 _____

tour **10**-7 _____

tour guide **10**-1 _____

tourist **10**-1 _____

tower **3**-4 _____

traffic **13**-1 _____

train **7**-6 _____

training **4**-1 _____

tram **13**-1 _____

transportation **6**-1 _____

travel **7**-1 _____

treasure **2**-1 _____

truck **7**-6 _____

truck driver **8**-1 _____

Uu

up **9**-8 _____

useful **2**-1 _____

useless **2**-1 _____

Vv

van **15**-7 _____

vet/veterinarian **1**-1 = a doctor for animals

virtual reality **7**-1 _____

visit **2**-1 _____

volcano **3**-5 _____

Ww

wait **13**-6 _____

wallet **14**-9 _____

watch **14**-9 _____

well **4**-5 _____

while **15**-1 _____

wild **3**-8 _____

winner **9**-1 _____

wonder **9**-1 _____

wonderful **4**-3 _____

wonderfully **4**-3 _____

wool **10**-10 _____

world **1**-1 _____

worse **3**T _____

worst **3**-8 _____

writer **8**-6 _____

Yy

yesterday **9**T _____

IRREGULAR VERB LIST	
Base form	**Simple past**
be	was/were
buy	bought
come	came
dig	dug
do	did
find	found
forget	forgot
give	gave
go	went
have	had
know	knew
meet	met
put	put
see	saw
take	took
teach	taught
tell	told
wake	woke
win	won